Make Blackout Poetry

ABRAMS NOTERIE, NEW YORK

Painter, a rope.

Paint the town red (Am.), a spree.

Pal (Gip.), a partner, friend; an accomplice.

Palaver (Gip.), to talk,

Pale-face, Indian name

Pall (Sea term), to stop. ... ment used to stop the motion of th

Palmetto State (Am.),

Palm off, to impose upo ... as to the quality of an article.

Palming, swindling or secreting small articles in the hands for the purpose of theft.

Palm oil, money given as a bribe.

Pam, the knave of clubs at the game of loo.

Pane or **Parney** (Gip.), rain.

Panel game (Am.), is worked by a thief in connection with a girl of the town, who lures men to a prepared room, which the thief enters by a concealed door or a moveable panel.

Panel-worker, the operators in the game above described.

Panhandle (Am.), the name applied to a district of West Virginia ... as it does in a strip between Pennsy ... is a similar division of Texas a ... name.

Panniki

Pannum ... e Latin *panis*; French, *pain*; ...

Pan out, ... gulch miners of shaking up "pay ... the grains of gold from the eart ... said to "pan out well" and the exp ... or any well-paying venture.

What is Blackout Poetry?

By John Carroll, founder of Make Blackout Poetry

Sometimes referred to as erasure poetry, blackout poetry is simply the act of removing or "blacking out" existing text to create a new meaning or message. There are a lot of different approaches to creating blackout poetry, but the easiest way is to pick up a pen and printed page and selectively cross out some of the words. The non-redacted text becomes your poem.

I was introduced to blackout poetry through Austin Kleon, whose book *Newspaper Blackout* is a series of poems made entirely from pages of the *New York Times*. Another influential artist of this genre is Tom Phillips, who published a book in 1980 titled *A Humument: A Treated Victorian Novel*. In his book, Phillips reconstructed the story of the original novel by painting or collaging over the text on each page and only leaving the words exposed that told his new story. Kleon's poems are succinct black and white artifacts, while Phillips' project is a sprawling, multicolored, and visually detailed. They represent two ends of the spectrum that is blackout poetry. It really is a limitless art form.

Creativity is a Muscle

Blackout poetry is equal parts visual art and literature. It attracts people who are word lovers, visual artists, designers, or all of the above. I made a blackout poem a few years ago that said, "Creativity is a muscle." I've seen blackout poetry open the door to creativity for so many people. Regardless of skill level, making blackout poetry is something that everyone can do.

The Best Things About Blackout Poetry

IT GENERATES UNEXPECTED IDEAS.

When we make blackout poetry, we're automatically tapping into our subconscious. While scanning a page of text, you start to make word associations and to piece sentences together. Ultimately, this allows you to generate ideas that you probably wouldn't think of while sitting in front of a computer screen.

IT'S THERAPEUTIC.

I started making blackout poetry when I was experiencing feelings of stagnation, boredom, and depression. My thoughts and emotions were tied in a knot. The words that I was drawn to for each poem were indicators of how I was feeling, whether I was aware of it or not. The process of creating blackout poems gave me a sneak peek into my own mind.

IT FORCES YOU TO BE PRESENT.

In an era of endless distractions, it's a struggle to focus on one thing at a time and be fully engaged. Blackout poetry offers an opportunity to escape by creating a space where you can be present with your thoughts and create something with your hands. And specifically, the act of crossing out words and the repetition of blacking out one line after another is soothing and centering.

Basic How-To

Essentially, there's no right or wrong way to make blackout poetry, but here's some direction to get you started:

SELECT A PAGE OF TEXT.
This book contains texts from a variety of sources: newspapers, pages from classic literature, illustrated dictionaries, and more. Each one represents different creative possibilities. Start with any page that speaks to you!

CHOOSE YOUR WORDS.
Perhaps the easiest way to begin is to skim the existing text and focus on a word that pops off the page the most. From there, look for other words above and below it that form an idea, an image, or an emotion. Circle these words with a pencil or fine tip marker.

BLACK OUT THE REST.
Make the words that you've selected for your poem stand out by crossing out the rest of the text with your marker. A thicker tip black marker gets the job done most efficiently. If you are using a permanent marker, slide a piece of paper underneath the page that you are working on, so that the ink doesn't bleed on to the next page.

Discover Your Style

The beauty of blackout poetry is that it opens the floodgates of experimentation. How many different ways can you black out a page? There are infinite possibilities. I started out with a page from a book and a Sharpie, but eventually I moved on to using acrylic paint and my blackout poetry evolved into a study of color and texture.

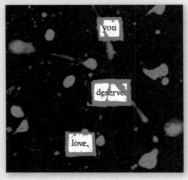

When I first began making blackout poetry, I was more focused on the words than I was on the visual possibilities.

Then I started applying heavy layers of acrylic paint to add color, depth, and texture to my poems.

Eventually, I discovered a whole new vocabulary of subtle effects by sanding down the layers of paint and creating more "air" around the text.

Experiment with structure

If you're accustomed to reading a page from top to bottom and left to right, initially your blackout poems may be constructed according to these conventions. However, you can also black out the page so that the words are read in a different order from their original context.

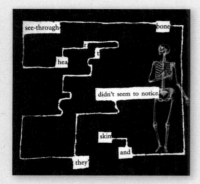

In this piece, the text is blacked out so that the words are connected by white lines (they look like ant tunnels), which direct the order in which the text is read.

Here, the artist creates two "stanzas" for this poem by dividing the page diagonally into two colored sections. The black area on top is read first, and the blue area below is read next.

Experiment with drawing and design.

If you love to draw or doodle, and if you have an eye for composition, then you can make blackout poems that are illustrative works of art.

The artist incorporates a drawing of her subject matter in the poem itself. Here she chooses not to black out the rest of the page, so you can read more of the original text.

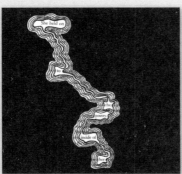

In this example, the visual flow of the selected words suggests an illustration. Is this a chain of isolated islands? An abstract diagram of the human digestion system? Your interpretation enhances the meaning of the poem.

Experiment with medium and dimension.

Who says that blackout poetry needs to be confined to paper and pen? This genre is all about transformation and innovation.

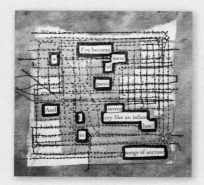

This multi-layered piece incorporates paint, marker, collage, and stitching to black out the original text—all used for visual and emotional impact.

Blackout poetry can be made without lifting a pen. This artist literally lifts words from a book by cutting them out with an X-acto knife and photographing the page to highlight the three-dimensional effect.

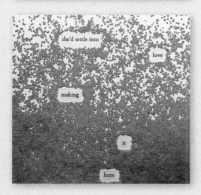

Another blackout poem in which no pen is required. This artist uses decorative sugar to highlight the words of her poem. Making impermanent compositions and capturing them in a photograph has profound implications for blackout poetry.

his mouth, and the other wants to stand up here and play the seer.' So the wooers spake in mockery, but neither Telemachus nor Odysseus paid heed to their words, for their minds were bent upon the time when they should take vengeance upon them.

XIV

IN the treasure-chamber of the house Odysseus' great bow was kept. That bow had been given to him by a hero named Iphitus long ago. Odysseus had not taken it with him when he went to the wars of Troy.

To the treasure-chamber Penelope went. She carried in her hand the great key that opened the doors — a key all of bronze with a handle of ivory. Now as she thrust the key into the locks, the doors groaned as a bull groans. She went within, and saw the great bow upon its peg. She took it down and laid it upon her knees, and thought long upon the man who had bent it.

Beside the bow was its quiver full of bronze-weighted arrows. The servant took the quiver and Penelope took the bow, and they went from the treasure-chamber and into the hall where the wooers were.

When she came in she spoke to the company and said: 'Lords of Ithaka and of the islands around: You have come here, each desiring that I should wed him. Now the time has come for me to make my choice of a man from amongst you. Here is how I shall make choice.'

Blackout Poetry
Plates

55. The sleepers are very beautiful as they lie unclothed,
   They flow hand in hand over the whole earth, from
      east to west, as they lie unclothed,
   The Asiatic and African are hand in hand — the
      European and American are hand in hand,
   Learned and unlearned are hand in hand, and male
      and female are hand in hand,
   The bare arm of the girl crosses the bare breast of
      her lover — they press close without lust — his
      lips press her neck,
   The father holds his grown or ungrown son in his
      arms with measureless love, and the son holds
      the father in his arms with measureless love,
   The white hair of the mother shines on the white
      wrist of the daughter,
   The breath of the boy goes with the breath of the
      man, friend is inarmed by friend,
   The scholar kisses the teacher, and the teacher kisses
      the scholar — the wronged is made right,
   The call of the slave is one with the master's call, and
      the master salutes the slave,
   The felon steps forth from the prison — the insane
      becomes sane — the suffering of sick persons is
      relieved,
   The sweatings and fevers stop — the throat that was
      unsound is sound — the lungs of the consumptive
      are resumed — the poor distressed head is free,
   The joints of the rheumatic move as smoothly as ever,
      and smoother than ever,
   Stiflings and passages open — the paralyzed become
      supple,
   The swelled and convulsed and congested awake to
      themselves in condition,
   They pass the invigoration of the night, and the
      chemistry of the night, and awake.

56. I too pass from the night,
   I stay a while away, O night, but I return to you
      again, and love you.

57. Why should I be afraid to trust myself to you?
   I am not afraid — I have been well brought forward

"Cinderella," said the Fairy, "I am your godmother, and for the sake of your dear mamma I am come to cheer you up, so dry your tears; you shall go to the grand ball to-night, but you must do just as I bid you. Go into the garden and bring me a pumpkin." Cinderella brought the finest that was there. Her godmother scooped it out very quickly, and then struck it with her wand, upon which it was changed into a beautiful coach. Afterwards, the old lady peeped into the mouse-trap, where she found six mice. She tapped them lightly with her wand, and each mouse became a fine horse. The rat-trap contained two large rats; one of these she turned into a coachman, and the other into a postilion. The old lady then told Cinderella to go into the garden and seek for half-a-dozen lizards. These she changed into six footmen, dressed in the gayest livery.

When all these things had been done, the kind god-mother touching her with her wand, changed her worn-out clothes into a beautiful ball-dress embroidered with pearls and silver. She then gave her a pair of glass slippers, that is, they were woven of the most delicate spun-glass, fine as the web of a spider.

When Cinderella was thus attired, her godmother made her get into her splendid coach, giving her a caution to leave the ball before the clock struck twelve.

On her arrival, her beauty struck everybody with won-der. The gallant Prince gave her a courteous welcome, and led her into the ball-room; and the King and Queen were as much enchanted with her, as the Prince conducted

Memoirs of Sherlock Holmes by Sir Arthur
Conan Doyle, published 1894
From: THE UNIVERSITY OF CALIFORNIA LIBRARIES

It was evening before we reached the little town of Tavistock, which lies, like the boss of a shield, in the middle of the huge circle of Dartmoor. Two gentlemen were awaiting us in the station—the one a tall, fair man with lion-like hair and beard, and curiously penetrating light blue eyes; the other a small, alert person, very neat and dapper, in a frock-coat and gaiters, with trim little side-whiskers and an eye-glass. The latter was Colonel Ross, the well-known sportsman; the other, Inspector Gregory, a man who was rapidly making his name in the English detective service.

"I am delighted that you have come down, Mr. Holmes," said the Colonel. "The Inspector here has done all that could possibly be suggested, but I wish to leave no stone unturned in trying to avenge poor Straker and in recovering my horse."

"Have there been any fresh developments?" asked Holmes.

"I am sorry to say that we have made very little progress," said the Inspector. "We have an open carriage outside, and as you would no doubt like to see the place before the light fails, we might talk it over as we drive."

A minute later we were all seated in a comfortable landau, and were rattling through the quaint old Devonshire city. Inspector Gregory was full of his case, and poured out a stream of remarks, while Holmes threw in an occasional question or interjection. Colonel Ross leaned back with his arms folded and his hat tilted over his eyes, while I listened with interest to the dialogue of the two detectives. Gregory was formulating his theory, which was almost exactly what Holmes had foretold in the train.

Would sweep the hedge away and make all plain,
Brilliant beyond all words, blinding the brain.

So the night passed, but then no morning broke,
Only a something shewed that night was dead,
A sea-bird, cackling like a devil, spoke,
And the fog drew away and hung like lead:
Like mighty cliffs it shaped, sullen and red,
Like glowering gods at watch it did appear,
And sometimes drew away and then drew near.

Like islands and like chasms and like hell,
But always mighty and red, gloomy and ruddy,
Shutting the visible sea in like a well,
Slow-heaving in vast ripples blank and muddy
Where the sun should have risen it streaked bloody;
The day was still-born; all the sea-fowl scattering
Splashed the still water, mewing, hovering, chattering.

Then Polar snow came down little and light,
Till all the sky was hidden by the small,
Most multitudinous drift of dirty white
Tumbling and wavering down and covering all,
Covering the sea, the sky, the clipper tall,
Furring the ropes with white, casing the mast,
Coming on no known air, but blowing past.

JOHN MASEFIELD.

***Through the Looking Glass and
What Alice Found There***
by Lewis Carroll, published 1897
From: THE NEW YORK PUBLIC LIBRARY

comes of having so many things hung round the horse——" So she went on talking to herself, as she watched the horse walking leisurely along the road, and the Knight tumbling off, first on one side and then on the other. After the fourth or fifth tumble he reached the turn, and then she waved her handkerchief to him, and waited till he was out of sight.

"I hope it encouraged him," she said, as she turned to run down the hill: "and now for the last brook, and to be a Queen! How grand it sounds!" A very few steps brought her to the edge of the brook. "The Eighth Square at last!" she cried as she bounded across,

　　　　*　　　　*　　　　*　　　　*　　　　*　　　　*

　　　　　*　　　　*　　　　*　　　　*　　　　*

　　　*　　　　*　　　　*　　　　*　　　　*　　　　*

and threw herself down to rest on a lawn as soft as moss, with little flower-beds dotted about it here and there. "Oh, how glad I am to get here! And what *is* this on my head?" she

Honolulu Star-Bulletin, published
September 21, 1917
From: THE LIBRARY OF CONGRESS

RODIEK MIXED UP WITH MAVERICK IS FEDERAL CHARGE

Alleged Conspiracy Activities of Then Acting German Consul Date Back to 1915 When "Mystery" Ship That Was to Carry Munitions to India Put Into Hilo

THAT the alleged connection of Georg Rodiek and Heinrich Augustus Schroeder with the plot to foment a rebellion in India dates as far back as 1915, when the steamer Maverick visited Hilo in the pursuit of its purported pro-German activities, is the information which has reached the Star-Bulletin from authoritative sources.

The information received by this paper throws further light on the recent arrest of Rodiek and Schroeder and clears up several points which have been held in doubt since the two Honolulu Germans left the territory to face trial in San Francisco.

The warrant of arrest was served on Rodiek after his arrival in San Franeisco, and that he knew he would be arrested when he reached that city is not now doubted. Rodiek was transferred to San Francisco for trial because a majority of the defendants involved in the Hindu conspiracy were residents of California, and it seemed expedient to the government to try all defendants in San Francisco rather than split the alleged conspiracy up into parts and carry on a number of trials.

The government's full case against Rodiek and Schroeder is withheld until their trial, but the Star-Bulletin

Single Check Brings $5000 To Red Cross

A visitor walked into the office of the Red Cross this morning and said he wanted to donate a small sum to the good work. The young lady in charge requested the caller to be seated, and she got out a book to enter a record of the donation.

"How much do you want to donate?" she inquired.

"Here's a check," replied the

Wild, vexed, cross, passionate, mad.

Wild-cat (Am.), country bank-notes of more than doubtful reputation. Also known as RED DOG and STUMPTAIL.

Wild oats (Eng.), youthful pranks, dissipation; fast young men are said to "sow their wild oats."

William, a bill.

Willow, a cricket bat.

Wilt, to wither, to droop.

Wind, empty talk, bragadoccio, gas.

Wind, "to raise the," to procure money.

Wind, "to slip one's," to die.

Windbag, a bloviant braggart.

Windfall, fruit shaken down by the winds. Also a slice of unexpected luck, or a legacy.

Windows, the eyes; poetically "the windows of the soul;" in slang known as "peepers."

Winey (Eng.), intoxicated.

Winged, shot in the arm or shoulder.

Winking, "like," very quickly.

Wipe, a handkerchief.

Wipe, a blow, to strike.

Wiped out, dead.

Wipe-out (Am.), to destroy or finish.

Wiping one's eye, taking a drink.

Wire, to telegraph.

Wire in, go in with a will; advice given by bystanders to a boy in a street fight.

Wire-puller (Am.), a political "fine worker," who sets up plans for the election of candidates and the passage or defeat of legislative measures.

Wire-pulling (Am.), political manipulation.

THE JOURNEY AND ARRIVAL

THE journey of Blondine lasted, as the Tortoise had said, six months. They were three months passing through the forest. At the end of that time she found herself on an arid plain which it required six weeks to cross. Then Blondine perceived a castle which reminded her of that of Bonne-Biche and Beau-Minon. They were a full month passing through the avenue to this castle.

Blondine burned with impatience. Would she indeed learn the fate of her dear friends at the palace? In spite of her extreme anxiety, she dared not ask a single question. If she could have descended from the back of the Tortoise, ten minutes would have sufficed for her to reach the castle. But, alas! the Tortoise crept on slowly and Blondine remem-

⚜ ⚜ ⚜ ⚜ ⚜ ⚜ ⚜ ⚜ ⚜ ⚜ ⚜

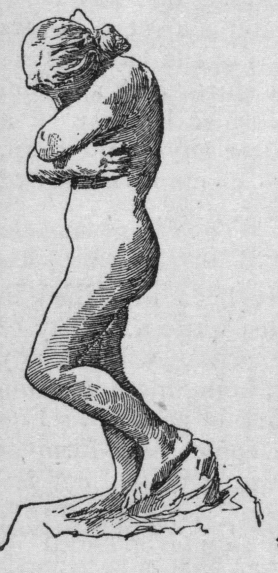

Eve.   Auguste Rodin, Sculptor.

IT was in this year, 1
began a bust of Roch
very beginning things
with the Red Republica
went on he became more
isfied, and finally would n
sittings.   His explanatic
ence at the sculptor's s
He says: "I went to t
morning, sat down reac
begin.   Then he would l
hour or two, turn to his
that for the same length
bullet of clay carefully o
time we were ready for
returning to the studi
through the same prelin
and then take off the b
never will be done."   T
his part, was equally dis
sitter's impatience and t
preciation, and, at last,
disgusted.   But the bulle
ittle story in the production of a great work of
Though not completed it was cast in plaster, and de
Rochefort's assistant editors and friends, not only a
out an astonishing piece of individualization.   Plaste
n the possession of several of the editors of Ro
L'Intransigéant.

So thou wilt woo; but else, not for the world.
In truth, fair Montague, I am too fond;
And therefore thou mayst think my 'havior
    light:
But trust me, gentleman, I 'll prove more true
Than those that have more cunning to be
    strange.   101
I should have been more strange, I must con-
    fess,
But that thou overheard'st, ere I was ware,
My true love's passion: therefore pardon me,
And not impute this yielding to light love,
Which the dark night hath so discovered.

Rom. Lady, by yonder blessed moon I swear,
That tips with silver all these fruit-tree tops,—

Jul. O, swear not by the moon, th' inconstant
    moon,
That monthly changes in her circled orb,   110
Lest that thy love prove likewise variable.

Rom. What shall I swear by?

Jul.   Do not swear at all;
Or, if thou wilt, swear by thy gracious self,
Which is the god of my idolatry,
And I 'll believe thee.

Rom.   If my heart's dear love—

Jul. Well, do not swear: although I joy in thee,
I have no joy of this contract to-night:
It is too rash, too unadvised, too sudden,

107. *"blessed moon I swear"*; so (Q. 1) Qq.; Ff. read *"moon I vow."*—I. G.

116 et seq. "With love, pure love, there is always an anxiety for the safety of the object, a disinterestedness, by which it is distinguished from the counterfeits of its name. Compare this scene with Act

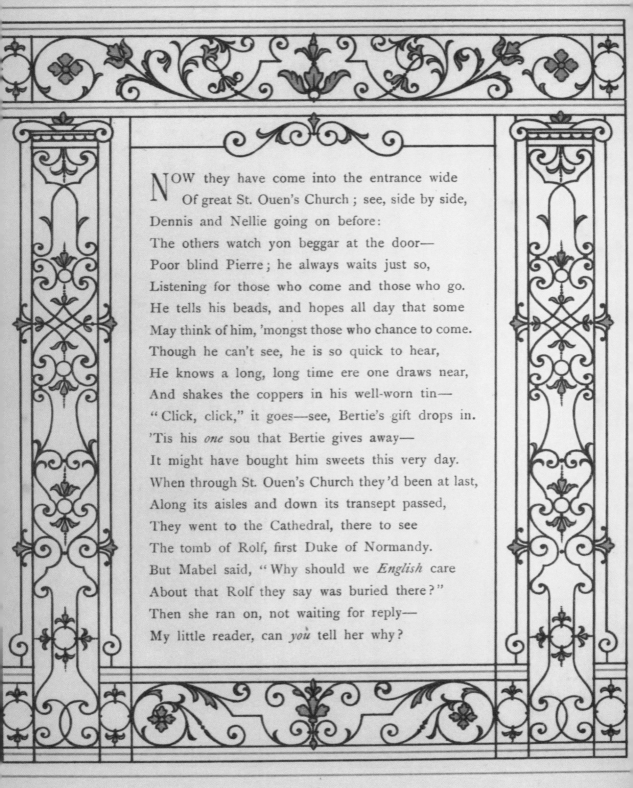

NOW they have come into the entrance wide
 Of great St. Ouen's Church ; see, side by side,
Dennis and Nellie going on before:
The others watch yon beggar at the door—
Poor blind Pierre ; he always waits just so,
Listening for those who come and those who go.
He tells his beads, and hopes all day that some
May think of him, 'mongst those who chance to come.
Though he can't see, he is so quick to hear,
He knows a long, long time ere one draws near,
And shakes the coppers in his well-worn tin—
"Click, click," it goes—see, Bertie's gift drops in.
'Tis his *one* sou that Bertie gives away—
It might have bought him sweets this very day.
When through St. Ouen's Church they'd been at last,
Along its aisles and down its transept passed,
They went to the Cathedral, there to see
The tomb of Rolf, first Duke of Normandy.
But Mabel said, "Why should we *English* care
About that Rolf they say was buried there?"
Then she ran on, not waiting for reply—
My little reader, can *you* tell her why?

Pride and Prejudice: A Novel
by Jane Austen published 1817
From: THE DUKE UNIVERSITY LIBRARIES

PRIDE & PREJUDICE.

———◆———

CHAPTER I.

It is a truth universally acknowledged, that a single man in possession of a good fortune must be in want of a wife.

However little known the feelings or views of such a man may be on his first entering a neighbourhood, this truth is so well fixed in the minds of the surrounding families, that he is considered as the rightful property of some one or other of their daughters.

"My dear Mr. Bennet," said his lady to him one day, "have you heard that Netherfield Park is let at last?"

Mr. Bennet replied that he had not.

"But it is," returned she; "for Mrs. Long has just been here, and she told me all about it."

Mr. Bennet made no answer.

VOL. I.   B   "Do

Daisy Bell

Arranged by
SYLVESTER KROUSE

Tune Ukulele
G C E A

Words and Music by
HARRY DACRE

Tempo di Valse

1. There is a flow-er with-in my heart, Dai - sy, Dai - sy!
2. We will go "tan-dem" as man and wife, Dai - sy, Dai - sy!
3. I will stand by you in "wheel" or woe, Dai - sy, Dai - sy!

Plant-ed one day by a glanc-ing dart, Plant-ed by Dai-sy Bell!
"Ped-'ling" a - way down the road of life, I and my Dai-sy Bell!
You'll be the bell which I'll ring you know! Sweet lit-tle Dai-sy Bell!

Wheth-er she loves me or loves me not, Some-times it's hard to tell;
When the roads dark we can both de- spise, P'lice-men and "lamps" as well;
You'll take the "lead" in each "trip" we take, Then if I don't do well;

10,008-2

orig. ed. cop. 1892

ing through the meshes of the hammock, he saw the Marches coming out, as if bound on some expedition.

"What in the world are those girls about now?" thought Laurie, opening his sleepy eyes to take a good look, for there was something rather peculiar in the appearance of his neighbors. Each wore a large, flapping hat, a brown linen pouch slung over one shoulder, and carried a long staff; Meg had a cushion, Jo a book, Beth a dipper, and Amy a portfolio. All walked quietly through the garden, out at the little back gate, and began to climb the hill that lay between the house and river.

"Well, that's cool!" said Laurie to himself, "to have a picnic and never ask me. They can't be going in the boat, for they haven't got the key. Perhaps they forgot it; I'll take it to them, and see what's going on."

Though possessed of half a dozen hats, it took him some time to find one; then there was a hunt for the key, which was at last discovered in his pocket, so that the girls were quite out of sight when he leaped the fence and ran after them. Taking the shortest way to the boat-house, he waited for them to appear; but no one came, and he went up the hill to take an observation. A grove of pines covered one part of it, and from the heart of this green spot came a clearer sound than the soft sigh of the pines, or the drowsy chirp of the crickets.

"Here's a landscape!" thought Laurie, peeping through the bushes, and looking wide awake and good-natured already.

It *was* rather a pretty little picture; for the sisters

Single Copies 6d.
Post free.

MARCH, 1916.

Annual Subscription, post free : Home, 5/-; Colonial, Foreign and American, 6/6.

Registered as a
Newspaper.

NEW SIX - SHILLING FICTION.

From all Libraries and Booksellers.

THE CRIMSON FIELD   Halliwell Sutcliffe

For the theme of this new romance Mr. Halliwell Sutcliffe has gone further back into English history than in any of his previous books, and, under the title of "The Crimson Field," gives us a vivid story of Flodden, that strangely varied battle, with its unusual contrasts, alternating superiority on either side, and the death of the Scottish King in the midst of the struggle. In the first historical romance of the modern school written on the period of that momentous conflict the author approaches Flodden Field with the march of the dalesmen of Wharfe to the scene of the fight, and shows their share in the last wild charge that settled the issue of the battle.

FREY & HIS WIFE (3/6) Maurice Hewlett

Mr. Maurice Hewlett's new work is a saga told with the wealth of detail and vivid actuality which have made the author's excursions into primitive Scandinavian history and legend as fascinating and as strongly human in their appeal as the mediæval romances which first made him famous.

FAITH TRESILION   Eden Phillpotts

A vivid story of love and high adventure on the Cornish coast. Mr. Phillpotts' books are quite unlike those of any other novelist, and his latest, strongly individual, is likely to prove itself one of the best novels of the year.

THE BORDERER   Harold Bindloss

Academy.—"This author's novels are terse, powerful, yet graceful, showing intimate knowledge and acute observation, never overweighted with description, yet containing many delightful pictures."

THE BROKEN THREAD William Le Queux

Mr. Le Queux can always be relied upon for a story crammed with excitement, and in this new tale, which concerns a vendetta and its workings, he is seen at his very best.

HUMAN NATURE   Marie Connor Leighton

Romance, mystery, and sensation, three ingredients skilfully blended as Mrs. Leighton alone knows how, go to make a most holding and engrossing story from this popular writer's pen.

THE SALT OF THE EARTH Fred M. White

Abounds in tense and exciting situations, and Mr. White's critics are of opinion that he has never written a better story.

THE ANNEXATION SOCIETY J. S. Fletcher

"Mr. J. S. Fletcher has certainly scored a record with his 'Annexation Society.' It is the most breathlessly exciting story that we ever remember to have read."—*Western Mail.*

BENTLEY'S CONSCIENCE   Paul Trent

Mr. Paul Trent's stories, "The Vow" and "The Foundling," were powerful tales with a motive. "Bentley's Conscience," as its title indicates, is of the same school.

THE INTERIOR   Lindsay Russell

This book is fresh proof that Lindsay Russell is a born story-teller; it glows with colour and emotion and contains a love story that will leave few readers unmoved.

THE WRAITH OF OLVERSTONE
Florence Warden

A really remarkable sensation story is Miss Warden's inimitable style—one whirl of thrills and incident.

THE FOOTLIGHT GLARE
Alice & Claude Askew

Alice and Claude Askew need no introduction as writers of powerful emotional stories, and in "The Footlight Glare" they have produced a vivid, rapidly moving and entrancing romance.

A DEBT DISCHARGED   Edgar Wallace

There is no lack of excitement in this brightly written novel, which holds the attention and interest of the reader to the end. The popular author of "Sanders of the River" again displays his gifts of originality and crisp dialogue.

WARD, LOCK & CO., LTD., Salisbury Square, London, E.C.

 # HOW TO BEHAVE AT A BANQUET

If a piece of MEAT crawls off your plate—CAPTURE IT AS SOON AS POSSIBLE and then gayly snap it across the table to your vis-a-vis. This will probably make EVERYBODY LAUGH and will help to make the meal quite MERRY.

If, inadvertently, you get a SPOT on the table-cloth, ABSENT-MINDEDLY PLACE A PIECE OF BREAD OVER IT, BUTTER SIDE DOWN. The BUTTER will keep the BREAD from slipping off the SPOT.

At any time when you happen to be drinking water—remember—it is considered quite a feat to make a gurgling sound like a SODA FOUNTAIN. This is quite a difficult thing to do but it will INVARIABLY ATTRACT an UNUSUAL AMOUNT of ADMIRING ATTENTION.

the side of the street with the Tannerie. At night, one could distinguish nothing of all that mass of buildings, except the black indentation of the roofs, unrolling their chain of acute angles round the place; for one of the radical differences between the cities of that time, and the cities of the present day, lay in the façades which looked upon the places and streets, and which were then gables. For the last two centuries the houses have been turned round.

In the centre of the eastern side of the Place, rose a heavy and hybrid construction, formed of three buildings placed in juxtaposition. It was called by three names which explain its history, its destination, and its architecture: "The House of the Dauphin," because Charles V., when Dauphin, had inhabited it; "The Marchandise," because it had served as town hall; and "The Pillared House" (*domus ad piloria,*) because of a series of large pillars which sustained the three stories. The city found there all that is required for a city like Paris; a chapel in which to pray to God; a *plaidoyer*, or pleading room, in which to hold hearings, and to repel, at need, the King's people; and under the roof, an *arsenac* full of artillery. For the *bourgeois* of Paris were aware that it is not sufficient to pray in every conjuncture, and to plead for the franchises of the city, and they had always in reserve, in the garret of the town hall, a few good rusty arquebuses. The Grève had then that sinister aspect which it preserves to-day from the execrable ideas which it awakens, and from the sombre town hall of Dominique Bocador, which has replaced the Pillared House. It must be admitted that a permanent gibbet and a pillory, "a justice and a ladder," as they were called in that day, erected side by side in the centre of the pavement, contributed not a little to cause eyes to be turned away from that fatal place, where so many beings full of life and health have agonized; where, fifty years later, that fever of Saint Vallier was destined to have its birth, that terror of the scaffold, the most monstrous of all maladies because it comes not from God, but from man.

It is a consoling idea (let us remark in passing), to think that the death penalty, which three hundred years ago still

Painter, a rope.

Paint the town red (Am.), to go on an extended spree.

Pal (Gip.), a partner, friend or accomplice.

Palaver (Gip.), to talk.

Pale-face, Indian name for a white man.

Pall (Sea term), to stop. A pall is a small instrument used to stop the motion of the windlass.

Palmetto State (Am.), South Carolina.

Palm off, to impose upon one by deceiving him as to the quality of an article.

Palming, swindling or secreting small articles in the hands for the purpose of theft.

Palm oil, money given as a bribe.

Pam, the knave of clubs at the game of loo.

Pane or **Parney** (Gip.), rain.

Panel game (Am.), is worked by a thief in connection with a girl of the town, who lures men to a prepared room, which the thief enters by a concealed door or a moveable panel.

Panel-worker, the operators in the game above described·

Panhandle (Am.), the name applied to a district of West Virginia from its shape, lying as it does in a strip between Pennsylvania and Ohio. There is a similar division of Texas and a railroad of the same name.

Pannikin (Old Eng.), a small pan.

Pannum (Gip.), bread. From the Latin *panis;* French, *pain;* Lingua-Franca, *pannen.*

Pan out, from the practice of the gulch miners of shaking up "pay dirt" in a pan to separate the grains of gold from the earth. If the dirt is rich it is said to "pan out well" and the expression is popularly used for any well-paying venture.

dreamed of the Sleeping Beauty and tried to break through her hedge, and, having failed, died there, and were forgotten by everybody except the tellers of fairy tales.

"Perhaps they felt as sure as I did," he thinks, sighing, "and they paid for being sure with their lives. Well, one can but try one's best, and there's a proverb I've heard since I came out of Fairy-land—'The many fail, the one succeeds.' Shall I be the one?"

His hands are on the thorn-branches, and they crash and break asunder before him until he has forced a way through the hedge that looked so impossible to overcome. The colour comes into his face as he hurries across smooth lawns and empty terraces, where every-thing is asleep but his shadow; up great steps and through long stone passages, with the hope of some-thing fair beyond all fairness flitting always before him, drawing him on as it had drawn him out of Fairyland, with a dream in the air before him and a whispering voice at his ear.

It draws him on till he is at last at the Princess's door; till, trem-blingly, he has pushed open its great oaken panels, inlaid with mother-of-pearl and tortoiseshell, and stands beside the golden couch where the pale Princess lies, with her black hair sweeping down to her feet.

The New President of France

The Rotogravure Picture Section of The New York Times next Sunday will include beautifully reproduced photographs of Deschanel, the new President of France, and Clemenceau, now in his 79th year, who was defeated in the recent election.

Other Photographs Next Sunday in

The New York Times

Admiral W. S. Sims giving his testimony before the Senate Sub-Committee on Naval Affairs, in which he charged failure of the Navy Department to support him.

Secretary of State Lansing exhibiting the original Constitution of the United States, shown for the first time in eighteen years.

Pope Benedict XV., taken in the beautiful halls of the Vatican during the public consistory attending the bestowal of the red hat on the new cardinals.

Professor Eamonn de Valera, "President of the Irish Republic," on the steps of the City Hall after having conferred on him by Mayor Hylan the freedom of the City of New York.

Statue of Christopher Columbus, made by Arnaldo Zocchi in Italy for the Argentine Republic. The statue, which weighs 200 tons, will be taken to Buenos Ayres aboard an Italian war ship.

unmixed delight. [*Rising and going to her.*] I am very fond of you, Cecily; I have liked you ever since I met you! But I am bound to state that now that I know that you are Mr. Worthing's ward, I cannot help expressing a wish you were—well just a little older than you seem to be—and not quite so very alluring in appearance. In fact, if I may speak candidly——

CECILY

Pray do! I think that whenever one has anything unpleasant to say, one should always be quite candid.

GWENDOLEN

Well, to speak with perfect candour, Cecily, I wish that you were fully forty-two, and more than usually plain for your age. Ernest has a strong upright nature. He is the very soul of truth and honour. Disloyalty would be as impossible to him as deception. But even men of the noblest possible moral character are extremely susceptible to the influence of the physical charms of others. Modern, no less then Ancient History, supplies us with many most painful examples of what I refer to. If it were not so, indeed, History would be quite unreadable.

CECILY

I beg your pardon, Gwendolen, did you say Ernest?

GWENDOLEN

Yes.

to pounce like a tiger, if the young man made any movement
to depart; and he only waited till the tavern should be clear of
company to effect the seizure.

Meanwhile, another person approached the young man. This
was the friendly stranger in the furred gown and flat cap, who
had sat next him at dinner, and who, it appeared, was not
willing to abandon him in his difficulties. Addressing him with
much kindness, the worthy personage informed him that he was
a bookseller, named John Wolfe, and carried on business at the
sign of the Bible and Crown, in Paul's Churchyard, where he
should be glad to see the young man whenever he was free to
call upon him.

"But I cannot disguise from you, Master Jocelyn Mounchensey
—for your dispute with Sir Francis Mitchell has acquainted me
with your name," John Wolfe said—"that your rashness has
placed you in imminent peril; so that there is but little chance
for the present of my showing you the hospitality and kindness
I desire. Sir Giles seems to hover over you as a rapacious
vulture might do before making his swoop. Heaven shield you
from his talons! And now, my good young sir, accept one
piece of caution from me, which my years and kindly feelings
towards you entitle me to make. An you 'scape this danger, as
I trust you may, let it be a lesson to you to put a guard upon
your tongue, and not suffer it to outrun your judgment. You
are much too rash and impetuous, and by your folly (nay, do
not quarrel with me, my young friend—I can give no milder
appellation to your conduct) have placed yourself in the power
of your enemies. Not only have you provoked Sir Francis
Mitchell, whose malice is more easily aroused than appeased,
but you have defied Sir Giles Mompesson, who is equally im-
placable in his enmities; and, as if two such enemies were not
enough, you must needs make a third, yet more dangerous than
either."

"How so, good Master Wolfe?" Jocelyn cried. "To whom
do you refer?"

SNEEZED HIS EYE OUT.

A Snuff Taker's Paroxysm Results in a Most Distressing Catastrophe to His Left Optic.

One of the most peculiar accidents ever recorded occurred the other day to Charles Doran, a resident of a Cincinnati suburb. Doran was nursing a severe cold, and, meeting a friend at the railway station, he accepted a proffered pinch of snuff. The membrane of his nasal passage was very delicate and sensitive, and he sneezed violently. So severe was the paroxyysm that the inferior oblique muscle of the left eye was ruptured, and, as he continued to sneeze, the exertion forced the eye completely out of the socket. A physician succeeded in replacing the eye in the socket.

Doran said, in describing his sensation, that the pain was not intense when the eye was forced out. He felt as though something was bursting in his head, but did not realize what had happened until he saw with his right eye that his left optic was dangling on his cheek. The pain of repairing the injury was much more severe than the injury itself.

THE LATEST IDEA IN WHEELS IS

Campaign (Am.), the period antecedent to an election, during which the candidates take the field, meetings are held and speeches delivered. The imagery of all such contests is taken from the battle-field.

Canard (Fr.), an unreliable story.

Canary, an English sovereign, from the color.

Candy-Butcher, an offensive nuisance, who accompanies traveling circuses, and peddles candy therein.

Canister (P. R.), the head.

Cannikin (Old Eng.), a small can. See Iago's song in *Othello*.

Canny (Scotch), clever, nice, neat.

Canoe (Am.), "to paddle one's own," is to go it alone; to make one's own way in the world.

Canon (Sp.), a narrow valley or passageway between rocks, often of great height. The Grand Canon of the Colorado is the largest known.

Cant, the slang of the Gipsies.

Cant (Eng.), a blow or a toss in wrestling.

Cant, to overturn; to throw.

Cantab (Eng.), a student at Cambridge University (*Cantabrium*).

Cantankerous, bad-tempered, litigious. Probably a corruption of contentious.

Canting, as applied to a professor of religion, means that he is a pretentious hypocrite. The word is said to have been derived from the name of one Andrew Cant, a Scotch clergyman, but this is extremely doubtful.

Cant of togs, a suit of clothes.

Canuck, a Canadian.

Canvaseens, sailors' trousers.

of loose skin and have transfixed it, for there are two little red points like pin-pricks, and on the band of her nightdress was a drop of blood. When I apologised and was concerned about it, she laughed and petted me, and said she did not even feel it. Fortunately it cannot leave a scar, as it is so tiny.

Same day, night.—We passed a happy day. The air was clear, and the sun bright, and there was a cool breeze. We took our lunch to Mulgrave Woods, Mrs. Westenra driving by the road and Lucy and I walking by the cliff-path and joining her at the gate. I felt a little sad myself, for I could not but feel how *absolutely* happy it would have been had Jonathan been with me. But there! I must only be patient. In the evening we strolled in the Casino Terrace, and heard some good music by Spohr and Mackenzie, and went to bed early. Lucy seems more restful than she has been for some time, and fell asleep at once. I shall lock the door and secure the key the same as before, though I do not expect any trouble to-night.

12 August.—My expectations were wrong, for twice during the night I was wakened by Lucy trying to get out. She seemed, even in her sleep, to be a little impatient at finding the door shut, and went back to bed under a sort of protest. I woke with the dawn, and heard the birds chirping outside of the window. Lucy woke, too, and, I was glad to see, was even better than on the previous morning. All her old gaiety of manner seemed to have come back, and she came and snuggled in beside me and told me all about Arthur. I told her how anxious I was about Jonathan, and then she tried to comfort me. Well, she succeeded somewhat, for, though sympathy can't alter facts, it can help to make them more bearable.

sh they will rot.

APRIL.

easure-ground and shrubbery,

DIELYTRA SPECTABILIS.

the hardy annual plants should be sown.

half-hardy shrubs are generally planted at this season. If they have been kept in pots, the ball of earth about the roots should be broken, and the roots carefully spread out before they are covered with earth, which should be to the depth of only from two to four inches, according to the soil; the greatest depth being necessary in the lightest soil. The Provence, white, and moss roses should now have their young shoots shortened to three or four buds; but the hybrid Provence roses should have five or six buds left; and the hybrid China, the Bourbon, and the Scotch roses, if intended for planting against a post, or a wooden frame, should have only the tips of their shoots taken off. The evergreen roses should be left at their full length; for if they are cut in they will produce long vigorous shoots, covered with an abundance of leaves, but having no flowers.

In the flower-garden, the early-flowering dwarf kinds of dahlia may be planted; and as the auriculas will now begin to flower, they should be shielded, if possible, from the effects of the weather. The hardy annuals that were sown in March in the open border should now be thinned, and the seeds of the re-In thinning the annuals

sycamore-trees — the flames — also the black
    smoke from the pitch-pine, curling and rising;
Southern fishermen fishing — the sounds and inlets
    of North Carolina's coast — the shad-fishery and
    the herring-fishery — the large sweep-seines —
    the windlasses on shore worked by horses — the
    clearing, curing, and packing houses;
Deep in the forest, in the piney woods, turpentine
    and tar dropping from the incisions in the trees
    — There is the turpentine distillery,
There are the negroes at work, in good health — the
    ground in all directions is covered with pine
    straw;
In Tennessee and Kentucky, slaves busy in the coal-
    ings, at the forge, by the furnace-blaze, or at the
    corn-shucking;
In Virginia, the planter's son returning after a long
    absence, joyfully welcomed and kissed by the
    aged mulatto nurse;
On rivers, boatmen safely moored at night-fall, in
    their boats, under the shelter of high banks,
Some of the younger men dance to the sound of the
    banjo or fiddle — others sit on the gunwale,
    smoking and talking;
Late in the afternoon, the mocking-bird, the American
    mimic, singing in the Great Dismal Swamp —
    there are the greenish waters, the resinous odor,
    the plenteous moss, the cypress tree, and the
    juniper tree;
Northward, young men of Mannahatta — the target
    company from an excursion returning home at
    evening — the musket-muzzles all bear bunches
    of flowers presented by women;
Children at play — or on his father's lap a young
    boy fallen asleep, (how his lips move! how he
    smiles in his sleep!)
The scout riding on horseback over the plains west
    of the Mississippi — he ascends a knoll and
    sweeps his eye around;
California life — the miner, bearded, dressed in his
    rude costume — the stanch California friendship
    — the sweet air — the graves one, in passing,
    meets, solitary, just aside the horse-path;

whose affection his hope of happiness was centred, yet of determined resolution to accomplish the object, if perseverance and energy could do it.

"LONDON, *February* 6, 1811.

"I wrote you a very hasty scrawl by an opportunity for Boston on the day of my arrival here, lest a knowledge of our unprecedented delays should have caused you anxiety.

"It is hardly possible to conceive such a series of untoward circumstances as I have met with since leaving Lisbon ; nor have my physical sufferings been inconsiderable, as you will perceive when I tell you that for six weeks of this uncommonly severe winter I have been quarantined on board my vessel and not allowed to have a fire. But that is past, and I will not trouble you with a recital of my discomfort, since I escaped being sick, which might have been expected as a consequence of such privations, and is a convincing proof that my constitution is restored to its pristine strength.

"During my confinement at Plymouth I wrote you several very long letters, and we have just learned that one of the vessels (by which I sent a large packet) has experienced a *warm* proof of the love Bony bears to Americans, as, with her cargo, she was burned at sea by the *Invincible Napoleon*, French privateer.

"Among the many extraordinary things which we daily see taking place in these extraordinary times Mr. Madison's proclamation of November 2 is certainly not the least singular.

"An English editor terms it 'a pretty specimen of republican sagacity,' and indeed I think it is ; for what proof has he of Bony's sincerity or good faith, that could justify such a measure? The event, no doubt, will show an error that will involve many in ruin.

"As it regards myself, if the silks I sent from Italy have not been sold, I have no doubt they will be more valuable than ever, as there is no prospect of a commercial intercourse with France. The American property which arrived there after November 1 has all been se-

his mouth, and the other wants to stand up here and play the seer.' So the wooers spake in mockery, but neither Telemachus nor Odysseus paid heed to their words, for their minds were bent upon the time when they should take vengeance upon them.

XIV

IN the treasure-chamber of the house Odysseus' great bow was kept. That bow had been given to him by a hero named Iphitus long ago. Odysseus had not taken it with him when he went to the wars of Troy.

To the treasure-chamber Penelope went. She carried in her hand the great key that opened the doors — a key all of bronze with a handle of ivory. Now as she thrust the key into the locks, the doors groaned as a bull groans. She went within, and saw the great bow upon its peg. She took it down and laid it upon her knees, and thought long upon the man who had bent it.

Beside the bow was its quiver full of bronze-weighted arrows. The servant took the quiver and Penelope took the bow, and they went from the treasure-chamber and into the hall where the wooers were.

When she came in she spoke to the company and said: 'Lords of Ithaka and of the islands around: You have come here, each desiring that I should wed him. Now the time has come for me to make my choice of a man from amongst you. Here is how I shall make choice.'

Dēēp'en (dē'pn), v. To make or become deep or deeper.

Dēēr, n. Wild horned ruminating animal of many species, hunted for its flesh, called *venison*.

Dēēr'skĭn, n. Skin of the deer, or leather made from it.

De-fāce', v. a. To destroy:—to disfigure.

De-fāce'ment, n. Act of defacing; condition of being defaced; that which defaces.

Deer.

Dĕf-al-cā'tion, n. Theft of money held in trust:—diminution.

Dĕf-a-mā'tion, n. Act of defaming; slander; calumny; detraction.

De-făm'a-to-ry, a. Slanderous.

De-fāme', v. a. To injure or destroy the reputation of; to slander.

De-fâult', n. Neglect; offence:—defect; lack.—2, v. n. To fail in a contract:—to fail to appear in court.

De-fâult'er, n. One guilty of default.

De-fēat', n. Overthrow; repulse:—frustration.—2, v. a. To overthrow; to conquer:—to frustrate.

De-fĕct', n. Deficiency; lack; imperfection.

De-fĕc'tion, n. Desertion; revolt; apostasy.

De-fĕc'tive, a. Having defects; deficient.

De-fĕnce', n. Act of defending; protection:—vindication; justification.

De-fĕnce'less, a. Exposed; unguarded.

De-fĕnd', v. a. To guard; to protect; to fortify:—to maintain:—to contest.

De-fĕnd'ant, n. One accused in a suit at law.

De-fĕn'si-ble, a. That may be defended.

De-fĕn'sive, a. Serving to defend:—resisting aggression.—2, n. State or attitude of defence.

De-fĕr', v. To put off; to delay:—to pay deference; to submit:—to refer.

Dĕf'er-ence, n. Submission:—high regard; reverence:—consideration.

Dĕf'er-ĕn'tial, a. Expressing deference; respectful.

De-fī'ance, n. Act of defying; challenge.

De-fī'ant, a. Full of, or expressing, defiance.—De-fī'ant-ly, ad.

De-fī''cien-cy (de-fish'en-se), n. Want or lack of a part or quality; imperfection; failure.

De-fĭ''cient (de-fish'ent), a. Wanting a

De-fīle'ment, n. Corruption; pollution.

De-fīne', v. a. To describe; to explain:—to fix the limits of.

Dĕf'i-nĭte, a. Precise; exact:—serving to define.—Dĕf'i-nĭte-ly, ad.

Dĕf-i-nī''tion (dĕf-e-nish'un), n. Act or process of defining; description or explanation of a thing by its qualities.

De-fĭn'i-tive, a. Positive; final.

De-flĕct', v. To cause to turn aside; to deviate; to swerve.

De-flĕc'tion, n. Deviation; a turning aside.

De-fôrm', v. a. To disfigure; to deface.

De-fôrm'i-ty, n. Want of beauty or symmetry, or of regularity;—that which deforms.

De-frâud', v. a. To cheat; to deceive.

De-frāy', v. a. To bear the expenses of.

Dĕft, a. Handy; skilful. [deceased.

De-fŭnct', n. Dead person.—2, a. Dead;

De-fȳ', v. a. To challenge:—to disregard; to brave.

De-ğĕn'er-āte, v. n. To be or grow worse; to decline.

De-ğĕn'er-ate, a. Having declined in worth; degraded.—2, n. One that has degenerated.

De-ğĕn-er-ā'tion, n. Act of degenerating; degenerate state.

Dĕg-lu-tĭ''tion (dĕg-lu-tĭsh'un), n. Act or power of swallowing.

Dĕg-ra-dā'tion, n. Act of degrading; degraded state; disgrace; debasement.

De-grāde', v. a. To lower in office, character, or value; to disgrace.

De-grād'ed, p. a. Debased; low.

De-grēē', n. Step or extent of movement in rank or attainment:—station; position:—step in relationship:—distinction conferred by universities and colleges:—360th part of a circle:—60 geographical miles.

Dē'i-fȳ, v. a. To exalt, praise, or worship as a god.

Deign (dān), v. n. To think fit; to condescend.—2, v. a. To grant:—to consider worthy.

Dē'ĭsm, n. Doctrine of a deist.

Dē'ist, n. One who believes in God, but not in revealed religion.

Dē'i-ty, n. Divine nature; divine Being; God:—heathen god or goddess.

De-jĕct', v. a. To dishearten; to discourage.

De-jĕc'tion, n. Dejected state; melancholy.

De-lāine', n. Thin dress material.

De-lāy', v. a. To put off:—to detain.—2, v. n. To linger; to procrastinate.—3, n. Postponement; a putting off; procrastination:—detention.

De-lĕc'ta-ble, a. Pleasing; delightful.

Dĕl-ec-tā'tion, n. Pleasure; delight.

Dĕl'e-gāte, v. a. To send as representative

I will slash at them!" he muttered to himself, and he gripped the hilt of his sword.

A tremendous hurrah was shouted behind him. "Only let me get at them!" And giving his horse a lift he spurred him to top-speed; the enemy were in sight. Suddenly a tremendous crack of whips lashed the whole line — Rostow raised his hand to strike with his sword, but at the same moment he saw Nikitenka, the man who was riding in front of him, gallop off out of sight, and he felt himself rushing on at a giddy pace, as if in a dream, without moving from the spot. A hussar flew past and looked at him with a gloomy face.

"What is happening? — I am not moving; have I had a fall? — Am I dead?"

Questions and answers buzzed in his brain. He was alone in the midst of a field; no frenzied horses, no hussars, nothing to be seen anywhere but the still earth and the short stubble. Something warm — blood — was flowing round him.

"No, I am only hurt; my horse is killed."

The "Crow" tried to get on to his feet, but fell back with all his weight on his rider; a stream of blood was flowing from his head, and he struggled in vain efforts to rise. Rostow attempting to get up also fell back; his sash had caught on the saddle.

"Where are our men? Where are the French?"

He could not imagine — not a soul was to be seen.

Having succeeded in freeing himself from the weight of his horse he got on his feet; where now was the line that so clearly divided the armies?

Expert Predicts Prosperity for 1921

Outlook for Business Good

IN a dispatch of the International News Service from Wellesley, Mass., Roger W. Babson, the well known statistician, tells why the business outlook in the United States is favorable.

"*First,* the working people in the country are in possession of the great majority of the bonds issued by the United States government during the war. This is a very favorable sign, for it shows that the great mass of people are in a sound financial condition.

"*Second,* that as a result of the coming of national prohibition two and one-half billion dollars previously wasted in this industry yearly is now available for business projects that are more useful and more likely to promote the welfare of the people.

"*Third,* that in spite of the widespread opinion to the contrary, the federal reserve banking system has been an important feature in stabilizing conditions in this country.

"*Fourth,* that advertising is now an influential means of moulding public opinion. This profession has now reached such an advanced and scientific stage in its development that it is a logical means by which the people of the country can be convinced that, contrary to their present opinion, business is really on a firm basis and that there is no cause for the present depression.

"*Fifth,* that the argument that the falling off of our foreign trade will prove ruinous is ill-founded, for such trade only constitutes 5 per cent. of the total. What little stoppage there is to be in this field, therefore, is of little or no consequence and will have no noticeable effect in the general business outlook.

"*Sixth,* that recently the standardization of manufacturing processes has been increasing with such amazing rapidity that there has been a considerable reduction in the cost of commodities. This is a permanent influence of no mean importance and should not be slighted in any consideration of the future of industries in general.

"*Seventh,* that all statistics gathered recently offer overwhelming proof that seasonal fluctuations in production in this country are rapidly decreasing. This will prove to be very beneficial, as it will tend to make the demands for labor more constant.

"*Eighth,* that taxation will be radically reduced in the near future.

"*Ninth,* that rapid progress is being made in industrial education with the result that the men employed in industrial plants are much better trained for their tasks and are performing them with far greater efficiency. The trade schools that are now established in all sections of the country are accomplishing wonders in this way.

"*Tenth,* that the United States as a result of the war is now a creditor nation instead of a debtor nation.

Charon the ferryman calleth, "What ho, wilt thou linger
      and linger?
Hasten—'tis thou dost delay me!" he crieth with beckon-
      ing finger.
    Admetus. Ah me! a bitter ferrying this thou namest!
O evil-starred, what woes endure we now!
    Alcestis. One haleth me—haleth me hence to the mansion
  Of the dead! dost thou mark not the darkling expansion
Of the pinions of Hades, the blaze of his eyes 'neath their
      caverns out-glaring?
What wouldst thou?—Unhand me!—In anguish and pain
      by what path am I faring!
    Admetus. Woeful to them that love thee: most to me
And to thy babes, sad sharers in this grief.
    Alcestis. Let be—let me sink back to rest me:
      There is no strength left in my feet.
        Hades is near, and the night
        Is darkening down on my sight.
        Darlings, farewell: on the light
    Long may ye look :—I have blessed ye
      Ere your mother to nothingness fleet.
Admetus. Ah me! for thy word rusheth bitterness o'er **me,**
  Bitterness passing the anguish of death!
Forsake me not now, by the gods I implore thee,
  By the babes thou wilt orphan, O yield not thy **breath!**
Look up, be of cheer: if thou diest, before me
  Is nothingness. Living, we aye live thine,
  And we die unto thee; for our hearts are a shrine
Wherein for thy love passing word we adore thee!
    Alcestis. Admetus—for thou seest all my plight—
Fain would I speak mine heart's wish ere I die.
I, honouring thee, and setting thee in place
Before mine own soul still to see this light,
Am dying, unconstrained to die for thee.
I might have wed what man Thessalian
I would, have dwelt wealth-crowned in princely halls;
Yet would not live on, torn away from thee,

" I might be a poor girl and welcome, and no matter, for Ronald loves me for myself, and will love me so for ever." She walked about her room as she spoke, and looked now at the dress and now at the veil she was to wear to-morrow as a bride.

Then she turned away from them to Alice, her old nurse, who had followed her into the room.

" Who went from here just now, my bird?" asked Alice.

" It was my cousin, Lord Ronald," said Lady Clare, smiling, and blushing. " He brought me a white doe, and that is the last gift he will give me as Lady Clare. After to-morrow what he gives me will be given to his wife."

Nurse Alice flushed too, but she did not smile. " Oh, God be thanked that all has come round so just and fair," she cried.

" What is this you are saying of justice and fairness, nurse? It is love and marriage between us two," said Lady Clare.

" I meant nothing else, my bird."

" Yes, you did. And I must needs know what you meant at once," said Lady Clare.

Alice wrung her hands. " Why will you want so old a story?"

" Tell me at once," said pale Lady Clare. And Alice trembled and told.

" I said ' Thank God that all has worked out so just and fair!' because—because—oh, child! Lord Ronald is not only heir of half the county, but he is master of all your lands as well, and you are not the Lady Clare."

" Are you gone mad?" said Lady Clare. And Alice wept and trembled more.

" By all that's good, I do but speak the truth at last. If you will have it—you are not the Lady Clare: you are my child. I was nurse to the old Earl's daughter, and she died in my arms, poor babe! I speak the truth as I live by bread! She died in my arms, and my baby girl was well and strong. I buried the old Earl's daughter like my own sweet child in the grave where my goodman lies, and I put my own child in her place. And nobody ever knew."

" That was a dreadful deed to do, mother," said she who was no

Trade and Literary Gossi[p]

Booksellers' Provident Institution.—We have delayed the issue of this month's "BOOKSELLER" in order to include a full report of the Annual Meeting, and of Mr. John Buchan's important address on "The Future of the War," which we are sure will prove specially interesting to our readers.

Mr. George Haven Putnam, the well-known publisher, has been elected president of the American Rights Committee, an organisation which has for its object the severing of diplomatic relations between the United States and the Teutonic Powers.

Buenos Aires.—Mitchell's English Bookstore and the English Book Exchange, 576, Cangallo, have purchased from the proprietor, Mr. W. C. Palmer, the goodwill and stock of the firm carrying on business under the name of the English Book Exchange. The business will in future be carried on under the title of Mitchell's English Bookstore and the English Book Exchange.

Leeds.—Messrs. Charles Henry Pickles, Ltd., of 117, Albion Street, Leeds, have acquired the wholesale newspaper and stationery business of Messrs. H. M. Trotter & Co., at Albion Court, Kirkgate, Bradford, and Royal Arcade, Fleece Street, Keighley.

The Religious Tract Society have arranged with Messrs. McClelland, Goodchild and Stewart, Ltd., Toronto, to carry a full range of samples of the Society's publications, and their travellers will wait upon the Canadian trade in due course.

Messrs. Williams & Norgate have increased the price of their "Home University Library," cloth binding, from 1s. net to 1s. 3d. net. The price in leather binding remains as before.

For King and Country.—T[he] been received since our last li[st]

MESSRS. W. H. SMITH & SON (H. Alty, 15th King's Liverpool; King's Liverpool; H. Izant, Ar J. S. Tanner, 11th Gloucester; Manchester; A. G. Jenkins, 15th G. A. Waterhouse, Royal West Ke Lancers; B. Hebbes, 3-8th Han 2nd Life Guards; A. Skilton, W Westlake, Royal Flying Corps; County of London; F. Kimp Brigade; C. Vardey, Royal Fusi London Irish Rifles; W. Champ London Royal Fusiliers; C. R. W Brigade; J. W. White, Army Se Edwards, East Surrey; S. C. Aylw R. Watkinson, Royal Flying Co Gloucester; H. S. Latcham, Col[d] Hamilton, Army Service Corps Oxford and Bucks L.I.; E. S. Wi of London Cyclists Corps; J. J. B. E. Lane, 14th County of Lon East Surrey; P. Gill, Coldstream London Rifle Brigade; G. Lo Brigade; C. H. Gibb, 15th Count Mitchell, Royal Fusiliers; G. T. H. W. Gray, North Stafford; J. H Derby; F. May, 12th Worcester; Westminster Rifles; G. Harding Gowers, Royal Marines; S. May A. E. Watts, King's Royal Rifle 11th County of London; G. Marines; Jas. Dobson, 3rd Buffs; of Wellington's; L. G. Matthe Rifles; H. Stevens, Royal West Royal Fusiliers.

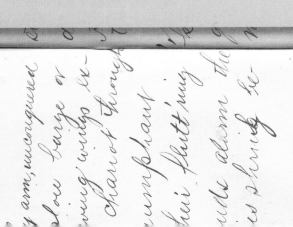

est woman, she is indeed more than I took
her for.   49

Lor. How every fool can play upon the word!
I think the best grace of wit will shortly
turn into silence; and discourse grow com-
mendable in none only but parrots. Go in,
sirrah; bid them prepare for dinner.

Laun. That is done, sir; they have all stom-
achs.

Lor. Goodly Lord, what a wit-snapper are
you! then bid them prepare dinner.

Laun. That is done too, sir; only 'cover' is the
word.

Lor. Will you cover, then, sir?

Laun. Not so, sir, neither; I know my duty.

Lor. Yet more quarreling with occasion!
Wilt thou show the whole wealth of thy wit
in an instant? I pray thee, understand a
plain man in his plain meaning: go to thy
fellows; bid them cover the table, serve in
the meat, and we will come in to dinner.

Laun. For the table, sir, it shall be served in;
for the meat, sir, it shall be covered; for your
coming in to dinner, sir, why, let it be as
humors and conceits shall govern.   [*Exit.*

Lor. O dear discretion, how his words are suited!
The fool hath planted in his memory   73

He opened it in the light of the coach-lamp on that side, and read— first to himself and then aloud: " Wait at Dover for Mam'selle.' It's not long, you see, guard. Jerry, say that my answer was, RECALLED TO LIFE."

Jerry started in his saddle. " That's a blazing strange answer, too," said he, at his hoarsest.

" Take that message back, and they will know that I received this, as well as if I wrote. Make the best of your way. Good-night."

With those words the passenger opened the coach-door and got in; not at all assisted by his fellow-passengers, who had expeditiously secreted their watches and purses in their boots, and were now making a general pretence of being asleep. With no more definite purpose than to escape the hazard of originating any other kind of action.

The coach lumbered on again, with heavier wreaths of mist closing round it as it began the descent. The guard soon replaced his blunder-buss in his arm-chest, and, having looked to the rest of its contents, and having looked to the supplementary pistols that he wore in his belt, looked to a smaller chest beneath his seat, in which there were a few smith's tools, a couple of torches, and a tinder-box. For he was fur-nished with that completeness that if the coach-lamps had been blown and stormed out, which did occasionally happen, he had only to shut himself up inside, keep the flint and steel sparks well off the straw, and get a light with tolerable safety and ease (if he were lucky, in five minutes.)

" Tom! " softly over the coach-roof.

" Hallo, Joe."

" Did you hear the message? "

" I did, Joe."

" What did you make of it, Tom? "

" Nothing at all, Joe."

" That's a coincidence, too," the guard mused, " for I made the same of it myself."

Jerry, left alone in the mist and darkness, dismounted meanwhile, not only to ease his spent horse, but to wipe the mud from his face, and shake the wet out of his hat-brim, which might be capable of holding about half a gallon. After standing with the bridle over his heavily-splashed arm, until the wheels of the mail were no longer within hearing and the night was quite still again, he turned to walk down the hill.

" After that there gallop from Temple Bar, old lady, I won't trust

of my story from me during the days of my lapse.

Very gently, when my mind was assured again, did they break to me what they had learnt of the fate of Leatherhead. Two days after I was imprisoned it had been destroyed, with every soul in it, by a Martian. He had swept it out of existence, as it seemed, without any provocation, as a boy might crush an ant-hill, in the mere wantonness of power.

I was a lonely man, and they were very kind to me. I was a lonely man and a sad one, and they bore with me. I remained with them four days after my recovery. All that time I felt a vague, a growing craving to look once more on whatever remained of the little life that seemed so happy and bright in my past. It was a mere hopeless desire to feast upon my misery. They dissuaded me. They did all they could to divert me from this morbidity. But at last I could resist the impulse no longer, and promising faithfully to return to them, and parting, as I will confess, from these four-day friends with tears, I went

Him let it view not, or it dies
Like tender hues of morning skies,
Or morn's sweet flower, of purple glow,
When sunny beams too ardent grow.

A charm o'er every object plays —
All looks so lovely while it stays,
So softly forth, in rosier tides,
The vital flood ecstatic glides,

That, wrung by grief to see it part,
Its dearest drop escapes the heart;
Such drop, I need not tell thee, fell
While bidding it, for thee, farewell.

LINES

COMPOSED AT THE REQUEST OF A LADY WHO RETURNED TO THE NORTH AND DIED SOON AFTER.

ADIEU, fair isle! I love thy bowers,
  I love thy dark-eyed daughters there;
The cool pomegranate's scarlet flowers
  Look brighter in their jetty hair.

They praised my forehead's stainless white;
  And when I thirsted, gave a draught
From the full clustering cocoa's height,
  And smiling, bless'd me as I quaff'd.

Well pleased, the kind return I gave,
  And, clasp'd in their embraces' twine,
Felt the soft breeze, like Lethe's wave,
  Becalm this beating heart of mine.

Why will my heart so wildly beat?
  Say, Seraphs, is my lot too blest,
That thus a fitful, feverish heat,
  Must rifle me of health and rest?

but keeps up the spirits of his people by his own valour and conduct, he shall never be deserted by them, nor find his foundations laid in a wrong place.

These kind of governments are most tottering and uncertain when the prince strains of a sudden, and passes, as at one leap, from a civil to an absolute power ; and the reason is, because they either command and act by themselves or by the ministry and mediation of the magistrate. In this last case their authority is weaker and more ticklish, because it depends much upon the pleasure and concurrence of the chief officers, who, in time of adversity especially, can remove them easily, either by neglecting or resisting their commands ; nor is there any way for such a prince, in the perplexity of his affairs, to establish a tyranny, because those citizens and subjects who used to exercise the magistracy retain still such power and influence upon the people, that they will not infringe the laws to obey his ; and in time of danger he shall always want such as he can trust. So that a prince is not to take his measures according to what he sees in times of peace, when of the subjects, having nothing to do but to be governed, every one runs, every one

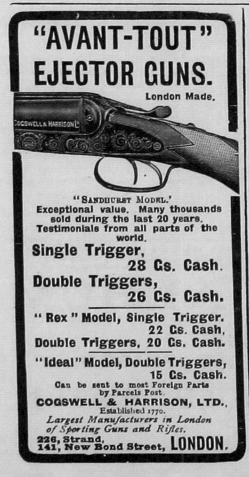

Corona Borealis, the **Northern Crown**, a smaller constellation east of and close to Bootes, west of Hercules, and just above the Serpent's head, is composed of a pretty semi-circle of six stars, supposed to form a chaplet or crown. The third nearest Bootes, the most brilliant, is *Alpherat*, a star of second magnitude.

North, Northeast.

The northern region, in strange contrast to the brilliant southern sky, shows no large stars and no prominent constellation is in good position for observation with the exception of *Cassiopeia*, or the Lady in the Chair, readily recognized by five stars (northeast, in the Milky Way), in the form of an open "straggling" **W**. It is on the opposite side of the Pole Star from the Dipper; a line drawn from the centre of the latter (where the handle joins the cup) through the Pole Star, about the same distance beyond it, will strike the last star of the **W**, which now is nearly upright (not reversed, as erroneously shown in map).

Auriga, the Charioteer, will rise later in the season in the north-eastern sky, where it will attract attention by its brightly scintillating star of first magnitude, called *Capella*, the Goat.

Capella rises in the latter part of July toward 11; middle of August to middle of September, between 10 and 8 P.M.

The Planets.

The planets, the restless wanderers, are easily distinguished from the fixed stars by their steady light, as they never, like the latter, twinkle or scintillate, except when very near the horizon.

"If that is so," said the child, joyfully, "I will ask them to carry me back to Kansas at once."

She threw her arms around the Lion's neck and kissed him, patting his big head tenderly. Then she kissed the Tin Woodman, who was weeping in a way most dangerous to his joints. But she hugged the soft, stuffed body of the Scarecrow in her arms instead of kissing his painted face, and found she was crying herself at this sorrowful parting from her loving comrades.

Glinda the Good stepped down from her ruby throne to give the little girl a good-bye kiss, and Dorothy thanked her for all the kindness she had shown to her friends and herself.

Dorothy now took Toto up solemnly in her arms, and having said one last good-bye she clapped the heels of her shoes together three times, saying,

"Take me home to Aunt Em!"

*   *   *   *   *

Instantly she was whirling through the air, so swiftly that all she could see or feel was the wind whistling past her ears.

The Silver Shoes took but three steps, and then she stopped so suddenly that she rolled over upon the grass several times before she knew where she was.

A phonograph for Christmas
—but what kind?

YOU'VE decided to give a phonograph for Christmas. But how will you decide *what kind* to give?

The owner of a "Crescent" Silvertone will tell you to buy one by all means. Yet it is neither fair, safe nor satisfying to buy a phonograph through hearsay.

There is a better way to choose—COMPARE the phonograph yourself with all other leading makes *before* you buy.

Compare it by playing the *same* record on each machine. Most machines are only made to play one *kind* of record. But you can play on each machine the record it was built to play. And no matter *what* kind of a record it is, you can play it again on a "Crescent" Silvertone.

The "Crescent" plays any and all disc records. No attachments to kill the tone. No adjustments. Just put the record on and play—*any* record, of *any* make, by *any* artist. You are not limited to a narrow group of records controlled by a single phonograph manufacturer. Your "Crescent" throws open the world's entire library of reproduction music. And it *makes the most of every record*. Your ear will tell you that.

This unlimited command of the best in music, with the finest and fullest reproduction of every record, will greatly multiply your pleasure in your Christmas phonograph. And there are many other "Crescent" features you would miss some day if you chose a phonograph at random.

Any "Crescent" dealer will demonstrate these features to you. All "Crescent" dealers will be glad to have you *compare* the "Crescent"—side by side, machine to machine, point for point, record for record and tone for tone—with any phonograph you have in mind.

In all fairness, *make* this comparison. THEN in buying the "Crescent" you will know first hand that you have chosen the Master Phonograph.

Ros. The hour that fools should ask.
Biron. Now fair befall your mask!
Ros. Fair fall the face it covers!
Biron. And send you many lovers!
Ros. Amen, so you be none.
Biron. Nay, then will I be gone.
King. Madam, your father here doth intimate
 The payment of a hundred thousand crowns;
 Being but the one half of an entire sum 131
 Disbursed by my father in his wars.
 But say that he or we, as neither have,
 Received that sum, yet there remains unpaid
 A hundred thousand more; in surety of the
  which,
 One part of Aquitaine is bound to us,
 Although not valued to the money's worth.
 If, then, the king your father will restore
 But that one-half which is unsatisfied,
 We will give up our right in Aquitaine, 140
 And hold fair friendship with his Majesty.
 But that, it seems, he little purposeth,
 For here he doth demand to have repaid
 A hundred thousand crowns; and not demands,
 On payment of a hundred thousand crowns,
 To have his title live in Aquitaine;
 Which we much rather had depart withal,
 And have the money by our father lent,

Through the Looking Glass and What Alice Found There
by Lewis Carroll, published 1897
From: THE NEW YORK PUBLIC LIBRARY

and set her on the table by the side of her noisy little daughter.

The Queen gasped, and sat down: the rapid journey through the air had quite taken away her breath, and for a minute or two she could do nothing but hug the little Lily in silence. As soon as she had recovered her breath a little, she called out to the White King, who was sitting sulkily among the ashes, "Mind the volcano!"

"What volcano?" said the King, looking up anxiously into the fire, as if he thought that was the most likely place to find one.

"Blew—me—up," panted the Queen, who was still a little out of breath. "Mind you come up—the regular way—don't get blown up!"

Alice watched the White King as he slowly struggled up from bar to bar, till at last she said "Why, you'll be hours and hours getting to the table, at that rate. I'd far better help you, hadn't I?" But the King took no notice of the question: it was quite clear that he could neither hear her nor see her.

Hotel Astor, "How to Behave at a Banquet", published 1914
From: THE NEW YORK PUBLIC LIBRARY, RARE BOOK DIVISION

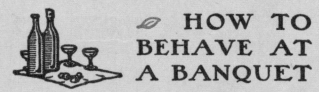

HOW TO BEHAVE AT A BANQUET

Managing a salad is VERY TRYING at times. It is so hard to eat one without getting MUSSED . UP . around . the MOUTH. We suggest leaving it alone. Don't LET ON that you are crazy to GET AWAY WITH IT. People will think that you have a DELICATE APPETITE, which is considered by many to be a mark of aristocracy.

If you bite your tongue—DON'T HASTEN TO UTTER A BUNCH OF BLUISH IDIOMS. It isn't NICE. Just let your tongue hang out of the corner of your mouth for a few moments until it has ceased being angry with you for having bitten it. In THIS DELICATE WAY you can apprise the people of your MISFORTUNE.

When pie is served—EAT THE HIDE AS WELL AS THE STUFFING. By doing this you will not cast REFLECTIONS on your host's PASTRY COOK.

Honolulu Star-Bulletin, published
September 21, 1917
From: THE LIBRARY OF CONGRESS

'I'll Come Back Another Time and Sing' Says Melba

Famous Opera Star Spends a Few Hours Here En Route to Mainland on Concert Trip

"GIVE my love to Honolulu and tell them that I am sorry I cannot stay this time and sing to the people of these beautiful isles," said Madame Melba, famous opera singer this morning on board the Canadian-Australian liner Niagara. Madame Melba is on her way to the United States for the coming opera season. She will sing in Chicago, Boston and New York.

"But tell them" she added, "that when I return this way I will stay a while and sing. I don't know when that will be. If the war is over in Europe in the spring I will go there, but if it isn't I will come back this way and sing for the folks here, for I love the islands and I love the people of these islands."

During the liner's short stay in port Madame Melba was taken about the city by H. B. Weller. She was accompanied by Lady Susan Fitzclarence of London, England, whose husband was killed on the battle field in France. Lady Fitzclarence is returning to her home after having paid a pleasure visit to Australia.

"You won't forget to give Honolulu my love, will you?" concluded Madame Melba as she stepped on the gangplank.

Saw 1300 of His Comrades Go Down At Neuve Chapelle

Captain Whose Regiment Was Wiped Out in Historic Battle Wins Cross

ONLY survivor today of the Royal Irish Rifles regiment which took part in the battle of Neuve Chapelle in October, 1914, nine weeks after war broke out and possessors of a military cross for his bravery in this engagement, Capt. L. Lindsay-Browne of London arrived in Honolulu today on the Niagara for a short visit to the islands. He is accompanied by his wife.

Capt. Lindsay-Browne was in England when the war broke out and while his career in the war was short in was full of excitement. His regiment went into the battle of Neuve Chapelle 1350 men strong and out of that number he was the only man to come out alive. The battalion held back the onsweeping Germans for four days following the great retreat from Mons.

"We were told to hold the line and we did for four days until the battalion was wiped out," said Capt. Lindsay-Browne. "We held it as long as we could and that's why I got the cross. The Germans took the point afterwards but we managed to straighten out the line and connect with the Belgians by holding them back. That's all," he

CHAPTER X

TWO PROMISES

MORE months, to the number of twelve, had come and gone, and Mr. Charles Darnay was established in England as a higher teacher of the French language who was conversant with French literature. In this age, he would have been a Professor; in that age, he was a Tutor. He read with young men who could find any leisure and interest for the study of a living tongue spoken all over the world, and he cultivated a taste for its stores of knowledge and fancy. He could write of them, besides, in sound English, and render them into sound English. Such masters were not at that time easily found; Princes that had been, and Kings that were to be, were not yet of the Teacher class, and no ruined nobility had dropped out of Tellson's ledgers, to turn cooks and carpenters. As a tutor, whose attainments made the student's way unusually pleasant and profitable, and as an elegant translator who brought something to his work besides mere dictionary knowledge, young Darnay soon became known and encouraged. He was well acquainted, moreover, with the circumstances of his country, and those were of ever-growing interest. So, with great perseverance and untiring industry, he prospered.

In London, he had expected neither to walk on pavements of gold, nor to lie on beds of roses; if he had had any such exalted expectation, he would not have prospered. He had expected labor, and he found it, and did it, and made the best of it. In this, his prosperity consisted.

A certain portion of his time was passed at Cambridge, where he read with undergraduates as a sort of tolerated smuggler who drove a contraband trade in European languages, instead of conveying Greek and Latin through the Custom-house. The rest of his time he passed in London.

Now, from the days when it was always summer in Eden, to these days when it is mostly winter in fallen latitudes, the world of a man has invariably gone one way — Charles Darnay's way — the way of the love of a woman.

He had loved Lucie Manette from the hour of his danger. He had

1,250,000 Horse-Power

for you

in horse-power hours is the daily average of electrical energy distributed throughout Manhattan by the generating plant of The United Electric Light and Power Co.

In factories and shops, large or small; in offices and homes—anywhere and everywhere it is necessary or desirable to save human energy—this electrical power lessens labor.

It lifts and hauls, it works ceaselessly to make possible a minimum expenditure of human effort. It contributes to your tremendous productions—it assures your safety, your welfare and your domestic happiness.

No matter what the nature of your power problems may be, our engineers are always ready to assist you in solving them. Their service entails neither cost nor obligation.

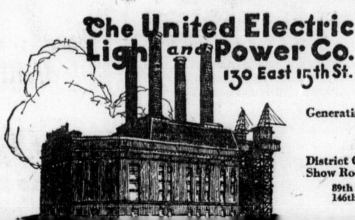

The United Electric Light and Power Co.
130 East 15th St.

Generating Station

West 201st Street and Harlem River

District Offices and Show Rooms

89th Street and Broadway
146th Street and Broadway

Dreaming of a day less dim,
Dreaming of a time less far,
When the faint but certain star
Of destiny burned clear for him,
And a fierce and wild unrest
Broke the quiet of his breast,

And the gristles of his youth
Hardened in his comely pow,
And he came to fighting growth,
Beat his bull and won his cow,
And flew his tail and trampled off
Past the tallest, vain enough,

And curved about in splendour full
And curved again and snuffed the airs
As who should say Come out who dares!
And all beheld a bull, a Bull,
And knew that here was surely one
That backed for no bull, fearing none.

And the leader of the herd
Looked and saw, and beat the ground,
And shook the forest with his sound,
Bellowed at the loathly bird
Stationed always in the skies,
Waiting for the flesh that dies.

Dreaming, this old bull forlorn
Surely dreaming of the hour

then went on as before. "For the sake of her child and her father, press upon her the necessity of leaving Paris, with them and you, at that hour. Tell her that it was her husband's last arrangement. Tell her that more depends upon it than she dare believe, or hope. You think that her father, even in this sad state, will submit himself to her; do you not?"

"I am sure of it."

"I thought so. Quietly and steadily have all these arrangements made in the court-yard here, even to the taking of your own seat in the carriage. The moment I come to you, take me in, and drive away."

"I understand that I wait for you under all circumstances?"

"You have my certificate in your hand with the rest, you know, and will reserve my place. Wait for nothing but to have my place occupied, and then for England!"

"Why, then," said Mr. Lorry, grasping his eager but so firm and steady hand, "it does not all depend on one old man, but I shall have a young and ardent man at my side."

"By the help of Heaven you shall! Promise me solemnly that nothing will influence you to alter the course on which we now stand pledged to one another."

"Nothing, Carton."

"Remember these words to-morrow. Change the course, or delay in it — for any reason — and no life can possibly be saved, and many lives must inevitably be sacrificed."

"I will remember them. I hope to do my part faithfully."

"And I hope to do mine. Now, good-by."

Though he said it with a grave smile of earnestness, and though he even put the old man's hand to his lips, he did not part from him then. He helped him so far to arouse the rocking figure before the dying embers, as to get a cloak and hat put upon it, and to tempt it forth to find where the bench and work were hidden that it still moaningly besought to have. He walked on the other side of it and protected it to the court-yard of the house where the afflicted heart — so happy in the memorable time when he had revealed his own desolate heart to it — outwatched the awful night. He entered the court-yard and remained there for a few moments alone, looking up at the light in the window of her room. Before he went away, he breathed a blessing towards it and a Farewell.

DOROTHY DIX'S LETTER BOX

Will He Be Happy Married to an Invalid?—Engaged to Two Women, Which Shall He Marry? — Robbing Mother of Son.

DEAR MISS DIX: I am a young man 25 years old, am poor, and have my way to make in the world. I am in love with a young woman who is everything that is lovely in womanhood, but she has never been well from her birth. She is weak and sickly. I don't believe that any one else would make the wife for me that she would, nor would I ever care as much for any other woman. But I do not want to marry trouble. What shall I do?

N. J. K.

Answer: I should certainly advise you to wait a while, and let nature take its course, as old-fashioned doctors used to say. Very often people who are sickly in their early youth gain strength as they grow older, and are healthy at middle age. Also, many diseases that used to be considered incurable fly away before the magic of modern science. Perhaps the young lady needs only some slight operation, or a course of treatment from some good doctor to be cured.

Take the girl to the very best diagnostician you can find, and let him find out what is the seat of her malady. Any one is foolish to submit to being a chronic invalid in these days when doctors and surgeons work so many miracles.

If your diagnostician gives an adverse verdict, and tells you that the girl will always be a semi-invalid, there are many things for you to consider before you marry her.

First is the money proposition, because sickness is the most expensive luxury on earth. Doctors and nurses and medicines are all bankrupting, and they are all things that we must have at any cost when one we love is suffering and calling to us for help.

An invalid wife is not only not a helpmeet to her husband, but she is a perpetual drain upon his pocketbook. It takes all he makes to pay her sick bills, and he has little chance to rise in the world.

Then look into your heart and see if your love is great enough to bear with patience the demands that an invalid is bound to make upon you. Sick people are not pleasant people to live with. It is only in novels that beautiful invalids, in lacy negliges, recline gracefully on couches, and bear their sufferings with a gentle, sweet smile. In real life they are nerve-wracked and cross and querulous and unreasonable, and only a sublime love can stand the exactions they make upon it.

Ask yourself if you will be willing to stay at home of evenings holding the hand of a sick wife, instead of going out with a jolly bunch; whether you can put up with slack housekeeping; whether you will enjoy tiptoeing in when you come home from work and find the house dark and wife in bed with her poor nerves; whether under such conditions you are sure you will never regret the bargain you made. And then act accordingly.

For it is undoubtedly true that the man or woman who marries an ~~invalid marries trouble.~~

DOROTHY DIX

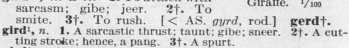

L'PEYS^z, pl.] [Scot.]
of either sex.
Scot.] To plunder;
n. [Scot.] A dis-
gill-rav'age‡.—

like gold. **II.** n.
perficial or mere-

ontrivance for al-
s compass, to tip
ng level, however
dim. of geminus,

I. a. Cheap and
< gim (< JUMP,
m'crack"er-y, n.
boring=tool with
w=tip. [< OD.^OF

flat, ornamental
etc. **gimp'ing**‡.
nd outlines in pil-
air=fillet.]
] **1.** To catch in
e the seeds from

) A machine for
. (2) A portable
d by a
are or
e", n.

oholic

B, lap; C, condenser.

brittle cake or bis-
=work, n. Cheap
y, a. Resembling

Cautious, or fas-
also adverbially.

tton dress=goods,
guingan, corr. of

ese tree cultivated

---

pardalis. **3.** [U. S.] A cage=like mine=car especially adapted for inclines. [F., < Ar.^Sp zarāf, giraffe.]

gir'an-dole, 1 jir'ən-dōl; 2 ḡir'an-dōl, n. **1.** A branching chandelier or bracket=light. **2.** A rotating firework; any rotating jet. **3.** Fort. A connection of several mines. **4.** A pendent piece of jewelry. [F., < L. gyro, turn.]

Gi-rard', 1 ji-rärd'; 2 ḡi-rärd', **Stephen** (1750–1831). An American banker; founded Girard College, Philadelphia.

gir'a-sol, 1 jir'ə-səl or -sōl; 2 ḡir'a-sōl or -sōl, n. Mineral. A bluish-white translucent opal with reddish reflections. **fire'=o"pal**‡. [F., < It. girasole, sunflower, turn (< gyro; see GYRATE, v.), + sole, sun, < L. sol, sun.] **gir'a-sole**‡.

gird[1], 1 gūrd; 2 ḡird, vt. [GIRD'ED^d or GIRT; GIRD'ING.] **1.** To bind around or about, as with a belt. **2.** To encompass; encircle. [< AS. gyrdan.]

gird[2d], vt. & vi. **1.** To attack with sarcasm; gibe; jeer. **2**†. To smite. **3**†. To rush. [< AS. gyrd, rod.] **gerd**†.

gird[1], n. **1.** A sarcastic thrust; taunt; gibe; sneer. **2**†. A cutting stroke; hence, a pang. **3**†. A spurt.

gird[2], n. [Scot.] A girth; a hoop. **girr**‡.

gird'er[1], 1 gūrd'ər; 2 ḡird'er, n. **1.** A principal horizontal beam, or a compound structure acting as a beam, receiving vertical load and bearing vertically upon its supports. **2.** One who or that which girds or encompasses. —**gird'er-age,** n. Girders collectively.

gird'er[2], n. A person who girds or gibes.

gir'dle, ⎱ 1 gūr'dl; 2 ḡir'dl. **I.** vt. [GIR'DL(E)D^D; GIR'-
gir'dl[P], ⎰ DLING.] **1.** To fasten a girdle or belt around. **2.** To encompass. **3.** To make an encircling cut through the bark of (a branch or tree). **II.** n. **1.** A belt used for girding a loose garment about the waist. **2.** Anything which encircles like a belt. **3**‖. A small band or fillet encompassing a column. **4.** Coal=mining. A thin sandstone stratum. **5.** Anat. The ring=like arrangement of bones, by which the limbs of a vertebrate animal are attached to the trunk. [< AS. gyrdel.]

girl, 1 gūrl; 2 ḡirl, n. **1.** A female infant or child, or a young unmarried woman. **2.** [Colloq.] A maid servant. [< LG. gör, child.]—**girl'hood,** n. The state or time of being a girl.—**girl'ish,** a. Like or pertaining to a girl. Syn.: see YOUTHFUL.—**girl'ish-ly,** adv.—**girl'ish -ness,** n.

girn, 1 gūrn or girn; 2 ḡirn or ğirn, vt. [Scot.] **1.** To grin. **2.** To growl or grumble. [gir'nel‡.

gir'nall, 1 gūr'nəl; 2 ḡir'nal, n. [Scot.] Same as GRANARY.

Gi"ronde', 1 ȝi"rônd'; 2 zhi"rôñd', n. The moderate republican party during the first French revolution (1791–1793). [< Gironde, a department of France.]—**Gi-ron'dist,** n. **Gi-ron'din**‡.—**Gi-ron'dist,** a. [girth of.

girt, 1 gūrt; 2 ḡirt, vt. & vi. **1.** To gird. **2.** To measure the

girt, 1 gūrt; 2 ḡirt, imp. of GIRD, v.

girt, pa. **1.** Naut. Moored so as to prevent swinging by wind or tide. **2.** Entom. Braced, as a chrysalis.

girth†, 1 gūrth; 2 ḡirth, vt. To bind as with a girth.

girth, n. **1.** A band or strap for fastening a pack or saddle to a horse's back. **2.** Anything that girds or binds.

Giraffe. 1/100

in the garden—a lovely little blue-eyed creature with yellow hair plaited into two long tails, white summer frock and embroidered pantalettes. The fresh-crowned hero fell without firing a shot. A certain Amy Lawrence vanished out of his heart and left not even a memory of herself behind. He had thought he loved her to distraction, he had regarded his passion as adoration; and behold it was only a poor little evanescent partiality. He had been months winning her; she had confessed hardly a week ago; he had been the happiest and the proudest boy in the world only seven short days, and here in one

"SHOWING OFF."

instant of time she had gone out of his heart like a casual stranger whose visit is done.

He worshiped this new angel with furtive eye, till he saw that she had discovered him; then he pretended he did not know she was present, and began to "show off" in all sorts of absurd boyish ways, in order to win her admiration. He kept up this grotesque foolishness for some time; but by and by, while he was in the midst of some dangerous gymnastic performances, he glanced aside and saw that the little girl was wending her way toward the house. Tom came up to the fence and leaned on it, grieving, and hoping she would tarry yet a while longer. She halted a moment on the steps and then moved toward the door. Tom heaved a great sigh as she put her foot on the threshold. But his face lit up, right away, for she tossed a pansy over the fence a moment before she disappeared.

The boy ran around and stopped within a foot or two of the flower, and then shaded his eyes with his hand and began to look down street as if he had discovered something of interest going on in that direction. Presently he picked up a straw and began trying to balance it on his nose, with his head tilted far back; and as he moved from side to side, in his efforts, he edged nearer and

great chamber and come to where my mother sits weaving yarn by the light of the fire. My father will be sitting near, drinking his wine in the evening. Pass by his seat and come to my mother, and clasp your hands about her knees and ask for her aid. If she become friendly to thee thou wilt be helped by our people and wilt be given the means of returning to thine own land.'

So Nausicaa bade him. Then she touched the mules with the whip and the wagon went on. Odysseus walked with the maids behind. As the sun set they came to the grove that was outside the City — the grove of Pallas Athene. Odysseus went into it and sat by the spring. And while he was in her grove he prayed to the goddess, 'Hear me, Pallas Athene, and grant that I may come before the King of this land as one well worthy of his pity and his help.'

III

BOUT the time that the maiden Nausicaa had come to her father's house, Odysseus rose up from where he sat by the spring in the grove of Pallas Athene and went into the City. There he met one who showed him the way to the palace of King Alcinous. The doors of that palace were golden and the door-posts were of silver. And there was a garden by the great door filled with fruitful trees—pear trees and pomegranates; apple trees and trees bearing figs and olives.

Strep. Shall I then ever see this?

Cho. Yea, so that many be always seated at your gates, wishing to communicate with you and come to a conference with you, to consult with you as to actions and affidavits of many talents, as is worthy of your abilities. [*To* SOCRATES.] But attempt to teach the old man by degrees whatever you purpose, and scrutinize his intellect, and make trial of his mind.

Soc. Come now, tell me your own turn of mind; in order that, when I know of what sort it is, I may now, after this, apply to you new engines.

Strep. What? By the gods, do you purpose to besiege me?

Soc. No; I wish to briefly learn from you if you are possessed of a good memory.

Strep. In two ways, by Jove! If anything be owing to me, I have a very good memory; but if I owe, unhappy man, I am very forgetful.

Soc. Is the power of speaking, pray, implanted in your nature?

Strep. Speaking is not in me, but cheating is.

Soc. How, then, will you be able to learn?

Strep. Excellently, of course.

Soc. Come, then, take care that, whenever I propound any clever dogma about abstruse matters, you catch it up immediately.

Strep. What then? Am I to feed upon wisdom like a dog?

Soc. This man is ignorant and brutish.—I fear, old man, lest you will need blows. Come, let me see; what do you do if any one beat you?

Strep. I take the beating; and then, when I have waited a little while, I call witnesses to prove it: then, again, after a short interval, I go to law.

Soc. Come, then, lay down your cloak.

Strep. Have I done any wrong?

Soc. No; but it is the rule to enter naked.

CHAPTER XXVIII.

Elizabeth's spirits soon rising to playfulness again, she wanted Mr. Darcy to account for his having ever fallen in love with her. "How could you begin?" said she. "I can comprehend your going on charmingly, when you had once made a beginning; but what could set you off in the first place?"

"I cannot fix on the hour, or the spot, or the look, or the words, which laid the foundation. It is too long ago. I was in the middle before I knew that I *had* begun."

"My beauty you had early withstood, and as for my manners—my behaviour to *you* was at least always bordering on the uncivil, and I never spoke to you without rather wishing to give you pain than not. Now be sincere; did you admire me for my impertinence?"

"For the liveliness of your mind I did."

"You may as well call it impertinence at once. It was very little less. The fact is, that you were sick of civility, of deference, of officious attention. You were disgusted with the women who were always speaking and looking, and thinking for *your* approbation alone.

WOMAN'S ENTERPRISE

Published in the Interest of the Club Women of Baton Rouge, La.

Official Journal Sixth District, Louisiana Federated Women's Clubs, Louisiana State Division, U. D. C.

Entered as second-class matter, October 14, 1921, at the postoffice at Baton Rouge, La., under the Act of March 3, 1879.

Address All Communications to Box 15.

BATON ROUGE, LOUISIANA, OCTOBER 1, 1922.

OUR BOY SCOUTS.

The highly efficient manner in which the Boy Scouts discharged their self-imposed duties during the meeting of Confederate Veterans should not be permitted to pass without public acknowledgment. Meeting every arrival, conducting to assigned places, assisting and guiding the infirm, running hither and thither wherever needed proved of inestimable value and was worthy of the fine little gentlemen they are. Their politeness, their gentleness to the old men won the hearts of all and proved that honor and chivalrous conduct is the rule of that gallant body. Citizens of Baton Rouge should be and most undoubtedly are exceedingly proud of our Boy Scouts.

TO GUIDE THE TRAVELER.

In most counties and parishes of the Union and at one time in this parish the tourist or traveler was guided in traveling by mile and index posts and now that roads are improved and travel increased such guides are more necessary than ever before and the Police Jury should investigate the subject and thus ascertain if such conveniences are necessary. There are a great number of cross roads and roads where roads fork that give travelers considerable trouble to select one desired. Doubtful it is if sev-

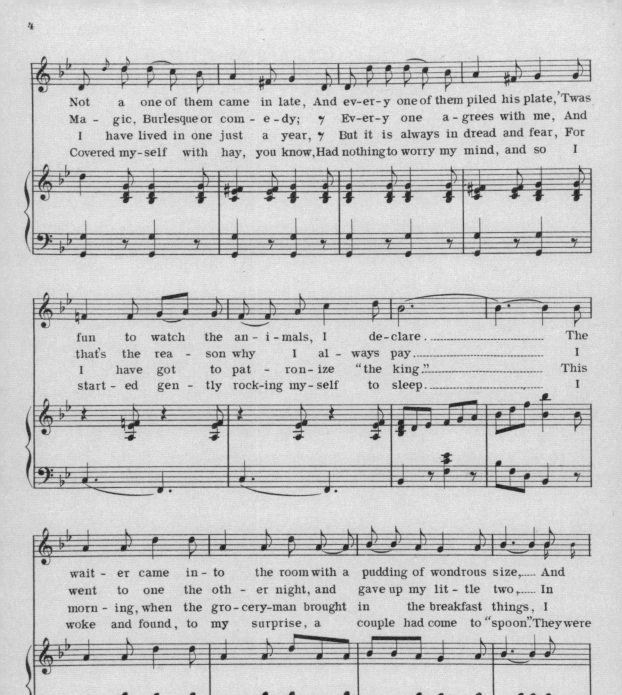

Not a one of them came in late, And ev-er-y one of them piled his plate, 'Twas
Ma - gic, Burlesque or com - e-dy; Ev-er-y one a-grees with me, And
I have lived in one just a year, But it is always in dread and fear, For
Covered my-self with hay, you know, Had nothing to worry my mind, and so I

fun to watch the an - i-mals, I de-clare. The
that's the rea - son why I al - ways pay. I
I have got to pat - ron-ize "the king." This
start - ed gen - tly rock-ing my-self to sleep. I

wait - er came in - to the room with a pudding of wondrous size, And
went to one the oth - er night, and gave up my lit - tle two, In
morn - ing, when the gro-cery-man brought in the breakfast things, I
woke and found, to my surprise, a couple had come to "spoon". They were

Sherlock Holmes laughed heartily. "We will come to that in its turn," said he. "I will lay an account of the case before you in its due order, showing you the various points which guided me in my decision. Pray interrupt me if there is any inference which is not perfectly clear to you.

"It is of the highest importance in the art of detection to be able to recognize, out of a number of facts, which are incidental and which vital. Otherwise your energy and attention must be dissipated instead of being concentrated. Now, in this case there was not the slightest doubt in my mind from the first that the key of the whole matter must be looked for in the scrap of paper in the dead man's hand.

"Before going into this, I would draw your attention to the fact that, if Alec Cunningham's narrative was correct, and if the assailant, after shooting William Kirwan, had *instantly* fled, then it obviously could not be he who tore the paper from the dead man's hand. But if it was not he, it must have been Alec Cunningham himself, for by the time that the old man had descended several servants were upon the scene. The point is a simple one, but the Inspector had overlooked it because he had started with the supposition that these county magnates had had nothing to do with the matter. Now, I make a point of never having any prejudices, and of following docilely wherever fact may lead me, and so, in the very first stage of the investigation, I found myself looking a little askance at the part which had been played by Mr. Alec Cunningham.

"And now I made a very careful examination of the corner of paper which the Inspector had submitted to us. It was at once clear to me that it formed part of a very remarkable document. Here it is. Do you not now observe something very suggestive about it?"

"It has a very irregular look," said the Colonel.

"My dear sir," cried Holmes, "there cannot be the least doubt in the world that it has been written by two persons doing alternate words. When I draw your attention to the

"That's the effect of living backwards," the Queen said kindly : "it always makes one a little giddy at first——"

"Living backwards!" Alice repeated in great astonishment. "I never heard of such a thing!"

"—but there's one great advantage in it, that one's memory works both ways."

"I'm sure *mine* only works one way," Alice remarked. "I ca'n't remember things before they happen."

"It's a poor sort of memory that only works backwards," the Queen remarked.

"What sort of things do *you* remember best?" Alice ventured to ask.

"Oh, things that happened the week after next," the Queen replied in a careless tone. "For instance, now," she went on, sticking a large piece of plaster on her finger as she spoke, "there's the King's Messenger. He's in prison now, being punished : and the trial doesn't even begin till next Wednesday : and of course the crime comes last of all."

While not an answering tone is heard,
   She spies a verdant olive tree;
And soon within that shelt'ring bower,
   She pours her very soul in song;
While other voices wake that hour,
   Her gentle numbers to prolong.

Thus, when this heart is sad and lone,
   As memory wakes her dirge-like hymn,
When Hope on heavenward wing hath flown,
   And earth seems wrapped in shadows dim —
O! then a word, a glance, a smile,
   A simple flower, or Childhood's glee,
Will each sad thought, each care beguile,
   Till joy's bright fountain gushes free.

To-day its waters gladly stirr'd,
   For Peace was nigh — that gentle Dove,
And sweet as song of forest bird,
   Came the low voice of one I love;
And flowers, the smile of Heaven, were mine,
   They whisper'd, "Wherefore art thou sad?
Of love, we are the seal and sign,
   We come to make thy spirit glad."

Thus, ever, in the steps of grief,
   Are sown the precious seeds of joy;
Each fount of Marah hath a leaf,
   Whose healing balm we may employ.
Then, 'mid life's fitful, fleeting day,
   Look up! the sky is bright above!
Kind voices cheer thee on thy way!
   Faint spirit! trust the God of Love!

ll gathered round the fire in the study—Mrs. Harker having
gone to bed—we discussed the attempts and discoveries of the
day. Harker was the only one who had any result, and we are
in great hopes that his clue may be an important one.

Before going to bed I went round to the patient's room and
looked in through the observation trap. He was sleeping soundly,
and his heart rose and fell with regular respiration.

This morning the man on duty reported to me that a little
after midnight he was restless and kept saying his prayers some-
what loudly. I asked him if that was all; he replied that it was
all he heard. There was something about his manner so sus-
picious that I asked him point blank if he had been asleep. He
denied sleep, but admitted to having "dozed" for a while. It is
too bad that men cannot be trusted unless they are watched.

To-day Harker is out following up his clue, and Art and Quin-
cey are looking after horses. Godalming thinks that it will be
well to have horses always in readiness, for when we get the
information which we seek there will be no time to lose. We
must sterilise all the imported earth between sunrise and sunset;
we shall thus catch the Count at his weakest, and without a
refuge to fly to. Van Helsing is off to the British Museum look-
ing up some authorities on ancient medicine. The old physicians
took account of things which their followers do not accept, and
the Professor is searching for witch and demon cures which
may be useful to us later.

I sometimes think we must be all mad and that we shall wake
to sanity in strait-waistcoats.

Later.—We have met again. We seem at last to be on the track,
and our work of to-morrow may be the beginning of the end. I
wonder if Renfield's quiet has anything to do with this. His
moods have so followed the doings of the Count, that the coming
destruction of the monster may be carried to him in some subtle

I followed this knight to a new castle outside this town, and came into the town asking for arms, but all your townsmen here are hawk-mad, and I could get no arms anywhere."

"So you are Geraint of Devon? Well, we know you by your renown, Enid and I," said the Earl. "As for the Sparrow-hawk, he is my own nephew, and he is like enough to be the knight whose dwarf struck your Queen's waiting-woman—like master, like man. I will not tell you his name, as you would fain have it from himself; but this I will tell you, that he desired to marry Enid, and being denied her, he raised my own town against me in the night, bribed my nearest friends and kinsmen, sacked my house and sent me here, a kind of prisoner, to this ruined castle, where he would kill me if he thought me worth the killing."

"Give me arms," exclaimed Geraint, "and I will bring his crest down to the dust."

"Arms I have," answered Yniol, "but old and rusty like myself, Prince Geraint. But no one can fight in this tournament except in the name of a lady, for the prize of the tournament is a golden sparrow-hawk, and the good knight who over-comes my nephew and carries off the hawk shall have the lady of his choice acclaimed as fairest of the fair. Have you a wife to fight for, Prince Geraint?"

"No," Geraint said; "but give me Enid for my wife, and I will lay lance in rest in her name, and if I live to bear away the prize she shall be Princess of Devon."

Then Yniol's heart danced in his bosom, because he saw that better days were coming for them all; and he called his wife to him, and took her hand in his.

"A girl is a tender flower, and

Bayou (Am.), a stream running out of instead of into a river, only possible in low, alluvial regions.

Bay State (Am.), Massachusetts.

Bazoo (Am.), "to blow one's" to boast or talk freely about oneself; to brag. In the "woolly West" there are a few frontier newspapers known as the "Bazoo."

Beach Combers (sea term), sailors on the Pacific coast.

Beak (Eng. or Gip.), a magistrate. Ancient Cant gives *Beck*, perhaps from the Saxon *Beag*, a gold collar emblematic of authority.

Beak-hunter, a poultry thief; derivation obvious.

Beam-ends. A ship thrown over on her side and in distress is on her beam-ends, and the term is applied to a man in trouble and poverty.

Bean-eaters, natives of Boston, Mass.

Beanpole, a very tall man.

Beans (Eng.), money. Probably from the French *Biens*, property.

Bear (Eng.), a Stock Exchange speculator who sells stock "short" which he does not possess and who speculates for a decline. See BULL. The name is probably derived from the old story about "selling the bear's hide before catching him," which is what the speculator for a fall actually does.

Bearing the market, trying to depress prices by selling large blocks of stock, gold, grain or other objects of speculation or by disseminating reports.

Bear-leader (Eng.), a private tutor to a young gentleman. As a corollary the pupil is known as a "cub."

Bear State, Arkansas.

Bearer-up (Eng.), a "capper" for a gambling house or mock-auction shop, who encourages others to speculate by playing or bidding-up as the case may be.

Beat, See DEAD-BEAT.

: THE FROG PRINCE :

I N the old times, when it was still of some
use to wish for the thing one wanted,
there lived a King whose daughters
were all handsome, but the youngest
was so beautiful that the sun himself,
who has seen so much, wondered each
time he shone over her because of her
beauty.   Near the royal castle there
was a great dark wood, and in the wood
under an old linden-tree was a well ; and when the day was hot,
the King's daughter used to go forth into the wood and sit by
the brink of the cool well, and if the time seemed long, she
would take out a golden ball, and throw it up and catch it
again, and this was her favourite pastime.

Now it happened one day that the golden ball, instead of
falling back into the maiden's little hand which had sent it
aloft, dropped to the ground near the edge of the well and
rolled in.   The king's daughter followed it with her eyes as it
sank, but the well was deep, so deep that the bottom could
not be seen.   Then she began to weep, and she wept and
wept as if she could never be comforted.   And in the midst
of her weeping she heard a voice saying to her,

"What ails thee, king's daughter ? thy tears would melt a
heart of stone."

And when she looked to see where the voice came from,
there was nothing but a frog stretching his thick ugly head
out of the water.

New York Hippodrome Souvenir Book, published 1917–18
From: THE NEW YORK PUBLIC LIBRARY, BILLY ROSE THEATRE DIVISION

Are You Enjoying Yourself?

(Written exclusively for the Hippodrome Programme by the Publicity Department, Liberty Loan Committee, Second Federal Reserve District.)

You probably lead a very satisfactory life in some ways and yet, behind the scenes, you may think that you are not having your share of the good things of earth. Yet you find time to go to theatres, and you wouldn't do this if the shows bored you. Summarize the argument by saying that, on the whole, things go pretty much according to your liking.

By way of contrast, try to realize the condition of your brother or your chum in the trenches in France. Try to visualize his daily routine—a rough march now and then, gun polishing, possibly a few hours between midnight and dawn peering over the top into No Man's Land. Almost anything would make him comfortable if it contributed a bit to his personal safety or ease, or to the waging of the great battle in which he is so tiny an item and yet so important a unit.

And while in this frame of mind, think of what you could do to make the lot of this man, or any one of a half million others similarly situated, somewhat easier. And then multiply any such exertion of effort on your part by ten millions, yes, even twenty millions. Then you will realize what extraordinary co-operation is demanded and what tremendous benefits will accrue from co-operation of this universal scope. But the chances to exercise such co-operation, except in spirit, are comparatively few. The average human mind appreciates it more thoroughly when the matter can be reduced to a material basis. Directly before us we have a chance to realize most fully the material aid that can be given by the co-operation of these ten or twenty millions.

The Third Liberty Loan gives us the opportunity. Every dollar you or your friends put into this great financial undertaking works overtime in behalf of the great cause of democracy —and incidentally in behalf of the man in the trench. If you have not already arranged to buy your share of these bonds, you cannot really be enjoying yourself.

Enter Puck.

Puck.   Through the forest have I gone,
But Athenian found I none,
On whose eyes I might approve
This flower's force in stirring love.
Night and silence.—Who is here?   70
Weeds of Athens he doth wear:
This is he, my master said,
Despised the Athenian maid;
And here the maiden, sleeping sound,
On the dank and dirty ground.
Pretty soul! she durst not lie
Near this lack-love, this kill-courtesy.
Churl, upon thy eyes I throw
All the power this charm doth owe.
When thou wakest, let love forbid   80
Sleep his seat on thy eyelid:
So awake when I am gone;
For I must now to Oberon.   [*Exit.*

Enter Demetrius and Helena, running.

Hel. Stay, though thou kill me, sweet Demetrius.
Dem. I charge thee, hence, and do not haunt me
    thus.
Hel. O wilt thou darkling leave me? do not so

the sum of that greatest velocity and the velocity in the ascent, and also their difference in the descent, decreases in a geometrical progression.

COROL. 3. Also the differences of the spaces, which are described in equal differences of the times, decrease in the same geometrical progression.

COROL. 4. The space described by the body is the difference of two spaces, whereof one is as the time taken from the beginning of the descent, and the other as the velocity; which [spaces] also at the beginning of the descent are equal among themselves.

PROPOSITION IV. PROBLEM II.

Supposing the force of gravity in any similar medium to be uniform, and to tend perpendicularly to the plane of the horizon; to define the motion of a projectile therein, which suffers resistance proportional to its velocity.

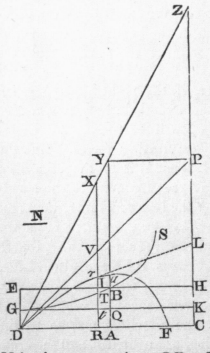

Let the projectile go from any place D in the direction of any right line DP, and let its velocity at the beginning of the motion be expounded by the length DP. From the point P let fall the perpendicular PC on the horizontal line DC, and cut DC in A, so that DA may be to AC as the resistance of the medium arising from the motion upwards at the beginning to the force of gravity; or (which comes to the same) so that the rectangle under DA and DP may be to that under AC and CP as the whole resistance at the beginning of the motion to the force of gravity. With the asymptotes DC, CP describe any hyperbola GTBS cutting the perpendiculars DG, AB in G and B; complete the parallelogram DGKC, and let its side GK cut AB in Q. Take a line N in the same ratio to QB as DC is in to CP; and from any point R of the right line DC erect RT perpendicular to it, meeting the hyperbola in T, and the right lines EH, GK, DP in I, t, and V; in that perpendicular take Vr equal to $\dfrac{tGT}{N}$, or which is the same thing, take Rr equal to $\dfrac{GTIE}{N}$; and the projectile in the time DRTG will arrive at the point r; describing the curve line DraF, the locus of the point r; thence it will come to its greatest height a in the perpendicular AB; and afterwards

Prince André made a face again and turned away. Pierre, whose merry, kindly eyes had been watching him ever since his entrance, now came up to him and took his hand. The prince's frown did not vanish at the sight of the new-comer; but when, a moment later, he recognized the frank face, his own lighted up with a cordial smile.

"Ah! you here, afloat on the tide of fashion!"

"I knew I should meet you here. I will go home to supper with you if I may?" He spoke low, not to interrupt Mortemart who was still speaking.

"No, you may not, of course," said André laughing, and wringing his hand to show how unnecessary the question was. He was about to say more, when Prince Basil and his daughter rose and there was a little stir to make way for them.

"Excuse our leaving you," said Prince Basil to the viscount, not allowing him to rise; "this tiresome ball at the English Embassy deprives us of a pleasure and compels us to interrupt you. I am so sorry, my dear Anna Paulovna, to be obliged to quit your delightful party."

Helen made her way among the seats, holding up her gown with one hand and never ceasing to smile. Pierre gazed at her dazzling loveliness in a rapture mingled with awe.

"She is very handsome," said Prince André.

"Yes," was all Pierre answered.

Prince Basil shook hands with him as he passed him.

4

folks said: "No; we have formed oth-er plans for you" ___ Then they
hope-less way through the bars of a cir-cus van, ___ But at

locked up the maid, for they felt quite a - fraid She'd e-lope and would soon be a
night as the light of ___ the moon-beams bright Steals in through the grat-ed

bride, But she danced on her tail in that home-made jail when she
door, How it lights up the gloom of his four-wheeled tomb When he

heard these ___ words out - side: ___ "Oh,
hears these ___ words once more: ___

THE DAY DREAM

THERE is a grey old Palace in the heart of the woods. It is lost like the forgotten answer to a riddle, and the very path to it is forgotten, for it is the Sleeping Palace. All around it the seasons are awake and busy at their work : grass-blades rise up in Spring, and sheaves are stacked in Autumn ; sap moves in the veins of the leaf, and misty vapour moves in the dip of a valley or combe ; but in the Sleeping Palace nothing moves at all. Nothing dies there ; nothing returns or is renewed.

The grey stone urns along the edges of the terraces never crumble ; the banner that droops on the flagstaff of the central tower never fades for wind or weather ; the fires on the hearths in the Palace rooms never go out, although no hand feeds them with wood or coal ; the peacock is asleep in the laurel-walk, and the parrot is asleep in his cage. Birds in the nests under the eaves sit sleeping on sleeping eggs ; in the closets mantles droop sleepily from their golden pegs, and the moth that has begun to eat them sleeps too. There is not even the thin note of a gnat to be heard, and the Sleeping Palace, full of live men and women, seems more like a picture than the pictures on its walls.

Live men and women, did I say ? Yes ; the Palace is full of men and women, every one of them alive, and every one asleep at work or play, just as the fairy spell touched them a hundred years ago.

The butler is in his pantry, with a flask of his master's wine

large piece suddenly came off and fell with a sharp noise that brought his heart into his mouth.

For a minute he scarcely realized what this meant, and, although the heat was excessive, he clambered down into the pit close to the bulk to see the thing more clearly. He fancied even then that the cooling of the body might account for this, but what disturbed that idea was the fact that the ash was falling only from the end of the cylinder.

And then he perceived that, very slowly, the circular top of the cylinder was rotating on its body. It was such a gradual movement that he discovered it only through noticing that a black mark that had been near him five minutes ago was now at the other side of the circumference. Even then he scarcely understood what this indicated, until he heard a muffled grating sound and saw the black mark jerk forward an inch or so. Then the thing came upon him in a flash. The cylinder was artificial—hollow—with an end that screwed out! Something within the cylinder was unscrewing the top!

'Good heavens!' said Ogilvy. 'There's a man in it—men in it! Half roasted to death! Trying to escape!'

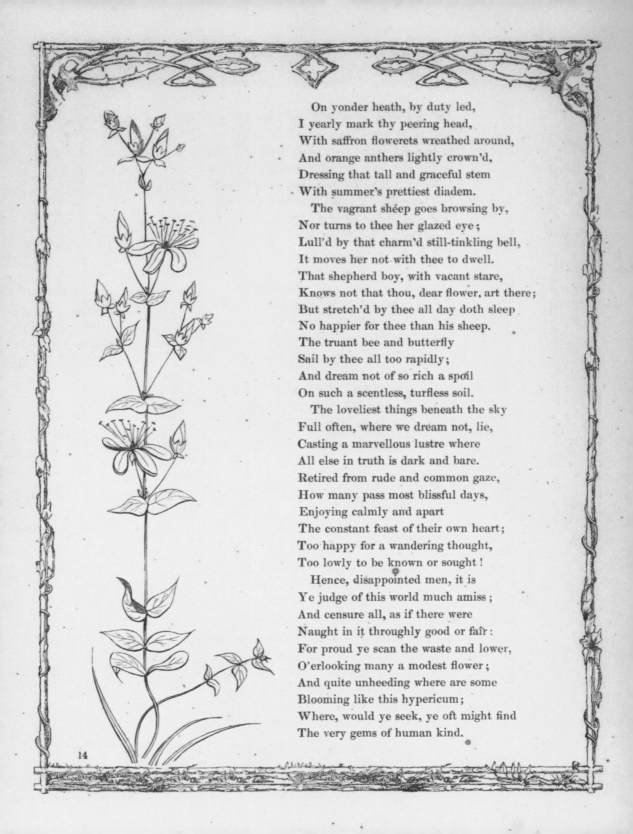

On yonder heath, by duty led,
I yearly mark thy peering head,
With saffron flowerets wreathed around,
And orange anthers lightly crown'd,
Dressing that tall and graceful stem
With summer's prettiest diadem.
  The vagrant sheep goes browsing by,
Nor turns to thee her glazed eye;
Lull'd by that charm'd still-tinkling bell,
It moves her not with thee to dwell.
That shepherd boy, with vacant stare,
Knows not that thou, dear flower, art there;
But stretch'd by thee all day doth sleep
No happier for thee than his sheep.
The truant bee and butterfly
Sail by thee all too rapidly;
And dream not of so rich a spoil
On such a scentless, turfless soil.
  The loveliest things beneath the sky
Full often, where we dream not, lie,
Casting a marvellous lustre where
All else in truth is dark and bare.
Retired from rude and common gaze,
How many pass most blissful days,
Enjoying calmly and apart
The constant feast of their own heart;
Too happy for a wandering thought,
Too lowly to be known or sought!
  Hence, disappointed men, it is
Ye judge of this world much amiss;
And censure all, as if there were
Naught in it throughly good or fair:
For proud ye scan the waste and lower,
O'erlooking many a modest flower;
And quite unheeding where are some
Blooming like this hypericum;
Where, would ye seek, ye oft might find
The very gems of human kind.

14

"Do you think Oz could give me courage?" asked the cowardly Lion.

"Just as easily as he could give me brains," said the Scarecrow.

"Or give me a heart," said the Tin Woodman.

"Or send me back to Kansas," said Dorothy.

"Then, if you don't mind, I'll go with you," said the Lion, "for my life is simply unbearable without a bit of courage."

"You will be very welcome," answered Dorothy, "for you will help to keep away the other wild beasts. It seems to me they must be more cowardly than you are if they allow you to scare them so easily."

"They really are," said the Lion; "but that doesn't make me any braver, and as long as I know myself to be a coward I shall be unhappy."

So once more the little company set off upon the journey, the Lion walking with stately strides at Dorothy's side. Toto did not approve this new comrade at first, for he could not forget how nearly he had been crushed between the Lion's great jaws; but after a time he became more at ease, and presently Toto and the Cowardly Lion had grown to be good friends.

During the rest of that day there was no other adventure to mar the peace of their journey. Once, indeed, the Tin Woodman stepped upon a beetle that was crawling along the road, and killed the poor little thing. This made

a. Without soul :—base ;

hy ; sane :—orthodox :—
-heavy :—thorough ; en-
y thing audible ; noise ;
ea or strait :—air-bladder
e.—3, *v. n.* To give a
to the ear :—to find the
oy the lead and line.—4,
make a sound :—to play
:—to celebrate by sound :
o find the depth of.

ving sound ; sonorous.—
nding ; sound emitted :—
at sea.

Liquid food made from
s, milk, &c., variously
vored.

tart :—sharp ; peevish.—
cid substance.—3, *v.* To
sour.

oring ; fountain :—origin.
ermented cabbage.

lt pickle, as of pigs' feet,
dip.—2, *v. a.* To steep in
w or plunge into water.—
as a bird on its prey.—
idden plunge.

pposite to north :—south-
the United States.—2, *a.*
oward south.—3, *ad.* In,
south.

Point midway between
—2, *a.* Of, in, from, or
t.—3, *ad.* In, from, or
t.

Storm from south-east.
a. Of, in, from, or to-
.—2, *ad.* In, from, or
t.

Of, in, from, or toward
[east.
ad. & a. Toward south-
n from south.

Of, in, from, or toward
n, from, or toward south.
f, in, from, or toward
utherner.

Native or inhabitant of
s of the United States.
Farthest south.

wŭd). *n.* Fragrant ever-

Sŏûth-wĕst'er-ly, *a.* Of, in, from, or to-
ward south-west.—2, *ad.* In, from, or
toward south-west.

Sŏûth-wĕst'ern, *a.* Of, in, from, or toward
south-west.

Sŏûth-wĕst'ward, *ad. & a.* Toward south-
west.

Souvenir (sôv'nēr), *n.* Memento.

Sôv'er-eign (*or* sŏv'er-in), *a.* Supreme in
power ; predominant :—efficacious ; effect-
ual.—2, *n.* Supreme ruler ; monarch :—
English gold coin, worth about $4.86.

Sôv'er-eign-ty (sŭv'er-in-te), *n.* Supreme
power ; high authority ; royalty.

Sŏŵ, *n.* Female pig.

Sōw (sō), *v.* [*i.* sowed ; *p.* sown *or* sowed.]
To scatter or plant, as seed :—to dissemi-
nate.

Sōwn (sōn), *p.* from *sow*.

Sŏў, *n.* Kind of sauce from Japan and
China ; bean from which it is made.

Spä, *n.* Mineral spring.

Spāce, *n.* Interval of distance or time :—
room ; expanse ; extension :—leisure.—2,
v. a. To arrange with spaces.

Spā'cious (spā'shus), *a.* Extensive ; roomy.

Spāde, *n.* Sort of shovel :—suit of cards.—
2, *v. a.* To dig up with a spade.

Spāde'bōne, *n.* Shoulder-blade.

Spāke, *v.* Old and poetic form of *spoke*.

Spăn, *n.* Space from the end of the thumb
to the end of the little finger, extended ;
nine inches :—extent of stretch :—that
which bridges a gap :—space of time :—
pair, as of horses.—2, *v. a.* To measure :
—to extend across.

Spăn'gle, *n.* Small plate of shining metal.
—2, *v. a.* To besprinkle with spangles.

Spăn'iard (spăn'yard), *n.* Native of Spain.

Spăn'iel (spăn'yel),
n. Sagacious long-
haired dog.

Spăn'ish, *n.* Lan-
guage of Spain.—
2, *a.* Relating to
Spain, its inhabi-
tants, or its lan-
guage.

Spaniel.

Spănk, *v. a.* To strike with the open hand.
—2, *v. n.* To trot smartly.—3, *n.* Blow
with the open hand.

Spănk'er. *n.* Hinder sail of a ship, rigged

was a watch, the face of which was opal, the back a carved sapphire and the glass diamond. This watch was always going, was never out of order and never required to be wound up.

Rosette heard her page at the door and followed him. On entering the salon she perceived Prince Charmant, who was awaiting her with the most lively impatience. He sprang forward to receive her, offered his arm and said with eagerness:—

"Well, dear princess, what did the fairy say to you? What answer do you give me?"

"That which my heart dictated, sweet prince. I consecrate my life to you as you have dedicated yours to me."

"Thanks! a thousand times thanks, dear and bewitching Rosette. When may I demand your hand of the king your father?"

"At the close of the chariot race, dear prince."

"Permit me to add to my first petition that of being married to you this very day. I cannot bear to see you subjected to the tyranny of your family and I wish to conduct you at once to my kingdom."

Rosette hesitated. The soft voice of the fairy whispered in her ear, "Accept." The same voice whispered to Charmant, "Press the marriage, prince and speak to the king without delay. Rosette's life is in danger and during eight

Other Extensions of Blackout Poetry

Making blackout poetry can also be a means to another creative end. You can scale your poems up or down, apply them to new surfaces, or repurpose them for other projects. Here are just a few ideas:

TURN IT INTO A CRAFT PROJECT.
I've seen blackout poetry bookmarks, stickers, buttons, magnets, and T-shirts. Make your poems wearable, usable, and a part of your environment.

USE IT TO SPARK MORE WORK.
David Bowie used a form of blackout poetry to come up with lyrics for his songs. You might use blackout poetry to generate the perfect opening line to a novel or short story. Or perhaps a blackout poem yields the subject matter of a painting or illustration.

MAKE IT THE BASIS OF A COLLABORATION.
Whether the goal is teambuilding or initiating a project to do with a friend, making blackout poetry with others brings about some fascinating results. You could make copies of a page, pass them around to different people, and witness the variety of poems that spring from the same text. You might start a poem and hand it off to someone else to finish. The things that you learn about your collaborator are more important than the poem itself.

Share Your Work—Here's How!

Making blackout poetry had such a profound impact on my life that I decided to create a community around this amazing art form. I wanted to use the power of the internet to find and showcase other blackout poets, but I also felt strongly about displaying my work and creating it with people in real life. Here are some ways that you can share your own blackout poems:

TAKE IT TO THE STREET. Due to the success of artists like Banksy and Shepard Fairey, street art has gained a lot of mainstream popularity in recent years. Wheat pasting is one way to display your art out in the world, but beware, if you don't have permission to post it on public or private property, you could get into trouble (if you get caught).

PARTICIPATE IN FREE ART FRIDAY. There's a really cool art movement happening around the world called Free Art Friday. Not all cities participate, but in Atlanta—where I live—it is bustling. Here's how it works: Make a piece of art. Hide it somewhere in your city. Snap a picture of it on your phone. Post it to social media with the appropriate hashtag for Free Art Friday in your city. Then watch as people come to claim your art!

SHARE YOUR WORK ON SOCIAL MEDIA. Last, but not least, posting your work to social media is probably the easiest way to share your work. By using the hashtag #blackoutpoetry on Instagram, you'll enable anyone who is looking for blackout poetry to find your work.

I started an Instagram account called Make Blackout Poetry, where I've been posting my own work and featuring other people's work as well.

I'd love to see what you do with this book and beyond, so please feel free to post it online with the hashtag #makeblackoutpoetry. I'll be sure to check it out!

Credits

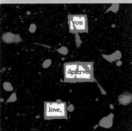

John Carroll (@makeblackoutpoetry)
Your life is not a small matter.

John Carroll (@makeblackoutpoetry)
You deserve love

John Carroll (@makeblackoutpoetry)
The impossible is inevitable

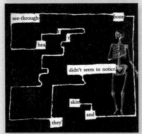

Nick Davies @waterwhispers
Skin and bone see-through heart they didn't seem to notice

Brenda Jette (@brenjet)
My lips must turn to despair. O!
Do not kiss by the book.

**Lynne Colette Love Hilliard
(@colette.lh)**
*I listen to the leaves and try to forget that World
within my head.*

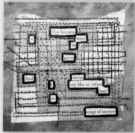

**Lynne Colette Love Hilliard
(@colette.lh)**
She held on to the poetry inside of her

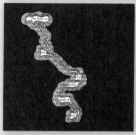

Heather Munro (@heathofthesea)
*I've become a mess of panic and terror. I cry like
an infant lost in songs of sorrow*

**Tiffany Taylor Brock
(@beautifullytwistedchaos)**
*Of course, we all fall
But we must try*

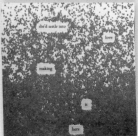

Leslie S. Nash (@laughinles)
She'd settled into love, making it hers

Design by Hana Anouk Nakamura

ISBN: 978-1-4197-3249-2

Text © 2018 John Carroll

© 2018 Abrams Noterie

Printed and bound in USA

10 9 8 7 6 5 4 3 2

Abrams Noterie products are available at special discounts when purchased
in quantity for premiums and promotions as well as fundraising or
educational use. Special editions can also be created to specification. For
details, contact specialsales@abramsbooks.com or the address below.

ABRAMS The Art of Books
195 Broadway, New York, NY 10007
abramsbooks.com